Controlling Collaboration between Firms

How to Build and Maintain Successful Relationships with External Partners

Controlling Collaboration between Firms

Ariela Caglio and Angelo Ditillo

AMSTERDAM • BOSTON • HEIDELBERG • LONDON
NEW YORK • OXFORD • PARIS • SAN DIEGO
SAN FRANCISCO • SINGAPORE • SYDNEY • TOKYO

CIMA Publishing is an imprint of Elsevier

CIMA Publishing is an imprint of Elsevier
Linacre house, Jordan Hill, Oxford OX2 8DP, UK
30 Corporate Drive, Suite 400, Burlington, MA 01803, USA

British Library Cataloguing in Publication Data
A catalogue record for this book is available from the British Library

978-0-7506-8131-5

For information on all CIMA publications
visit our website at books.elsevier.com

Typeset by Charon Tec Ltd., A Macmillan Company.
(www.macmillansolutions.com)

Printed and bound in Hungary

08   09   10   11   10   9   8   7   6   5   4   3   2   1

Working together to grow
libraries in developing countries

www.elsevier.com | www.bookaid.org | www.sabre.org

ELSEVIER   BOOK AID
            International   Sabre Foundation

To those who fulfil our lives with joy and love

Gianmarco and Pietro

Mamma, Papà and my whole family

Contents

List of Figures

List of Tables

Preface

As markets are becoming more and more globalised and are dealing with increased competition, firms are struggling to succeed in all the dimensions of business ventures. Only few firms are endowed with all the resources and capabilities necessary to operate in the market. All the others start to collaborate with other companies and become part of shared agreements with partner firms. In practice, such inter-firm associations – loosely mixing characteristics of the integrated firm and the free market – get instantiated into different forms such as subcontracting, supply-chain arrangements, franchising, licensing, strategic partnerships and diverse forms of alliances between firms such as joint ventures.

Such agreements have attracted the attention of both managers and academics for two important reasons. First of all, because they provide different management challenges than those found in conventional organisations. Secondly, because they have unique features that defy the descriptive and explanatory potential of extant theory, thus requiring further research developments.

The purpose of this book is therefore to explore these collaborative, inter-organisational agreements for substantiating their specific properties as governance and control structures. In developing our analysis, two tracks will be pursued. The first aim is to clarify in which sense the peculiarities of these arrangements raise unaddressed issues regarding their functioning. In fact, as firms set up various forms of collaborations and alliances to gain access to both scarce and dispersed resources and idiosyncratic capabilities, they require specific forms of relationship management that are able to generate steadiness and to retain the underlying economic and competitive advantages. The second one is to explain the challenges that new, collaborative forms of organisation have opened up to how management control systems and accounting information exchanges should be practised and designed, as necessary management tools to build and maintain successful relationships with external partners. More specifically, the objectives will be:

- to understand the hybrid nature of the governance structure (between markets and hierarchies) of collaborative partnerships;
- to illustrate the variables that explain the choice of different control modes in the various contexts of collaboration;
- to describe the characteristics of management accounting mechanisms for cross-boundary settings: collaborative programs and budgets, inter-firm

performance measurement systems and inter-organisational cost management techniques;

- to propose a network-based approach to management accounting, based on the novel concept of Accounting Information Network (AIN);
- to illustrate empirical evidence on control choices, management accounting practices and management accountants' role in these new collaborative organisational solutions;
- to present a generalisable framework on control and AIN choices in collaborative settings as a basis for providing some recommendations and guidance to practitioners operating inter-firm collaborative settings.

The book is arranged in six chapters. The first three chapters describe the characteristics of collaborative agreements between firms – legal forms, rationales for their formation and governance structures – highlighting their peculiarities in terms of management features and control problems. The fourth chapter of the book shows the reader the use of control mechanisms across organisational boundaries and their determinants. The fifth chapter contains a description of the management accounting practices suitable for boundary-spanning contexts and introduces a network-based approach to management accounting. Finally, in the sixth chapter, control and accounting information sharing practices are illustrated by means of data taken from a field study and from case studies developed around real business examples of successful inter-organisational collaborative relationships. More specifically, the focus is on fashion firms, which can be considered at the forefront experimentation with these new organisational solutions. In fact, in the fashion industry, firms normally outsource non-core activities and enter into shared, cooperative agreements with partners to carry out their operations. These firms are also particularly interesting because they have been recently revising their forms of collaboration along the value chain due the need to reduce their delivery times and costs, while at the same time maintaining high product quality and variety. Therefore, they are rethinking their way of stabilising and controlling the relationships with their collaborators, making their investigation particularly appealing to our ends. Chapter 6 concludes with the presentation of a framework for interpreting the empirical data collected, and provide some recommendations and guidelines on how to design control systems and AINs in collaborative settings.

As a final note, it is worth mentioning here that although this book is the result of a joint research effort of the two authors, we acknowledge that Ariela Caglio has taken charge of writing Chapters 3 and 5, while Angelo Ditillo of

Chapters 1, 2 and 4. The Preface and Chapter 6 have been developed in collaboration by the two authors.

We would like to express gratitude to CIMA for their financial support, thanks to which we could conduct our research and produce this book. In addition, we are also grateful to all those we involved in the project for their time and contribution to the development of the empirical part.

Collaboration between firms

In this chapter, we define the object of analysis of this book, that is to say the various forms of collaboration established between firms. More specifically, the purpose is to give an overview of all the forms that collaborative agreements may take.

The variety of cooperative forms

Many firms increasingly cooperate with other firms to coordinate the production of complex products and the provision of composite services in uncertain and competitive environments. This cooperation is widely seen as producing important economic advantages to organisations. Different forms of cooperation have been described. However, little attempt has been made to provide an integrative framework to classify these forms and describe their legal, strategic and organisational properties. Two studies that seem to be particularly comprehensive and therefore useful to present an overview of these inter-organisational collaboration associations are the ones by Grandori and Soda (1995: 198–205) and Grandori (1997: 910–918), who classify them according to whether the relationships are formalised or not (due to the support of exchange or associational formal contracts) and whether they are centralised (there is a central coordinating firm) or parity based.

Social collaboration forms

These inter-firm collaboration relationships include purely social links, which are not coupled with formal agreements. They need neither to be dedicated just to the exchange of 'social goods' such as prestige and status, friendship and sense of belonging, power and career opportunities, nor they need to be based on parity. Social influences can be reciprocal and include elements of leadership and authority in both inter-firm and interpersonal relations.

What follows is a presentation of symmetric or parity-based inter-firm relationships (Grandori and Soda, 1995; Grandori, 1997):

(1) *Personal inter-firm relationships* refer to links between firms through contacts among their entrepreneurs and managers. They often have exploratory purposes for the exchange of confidential information which has potential economic value (Schrader, 1991). These personal relationships, in which a firm is involved through its members, are crucial for maintaining a reasonably large and varied pool of trustworthy potential partners among which to search for more tightly coupled action-oriented networks (Granovetter,

1985; Aldrich and Glinov, 1990). They are also useful in context where there are problems of occupational mobility (Burt, 1980; Breiger, 1981), resource mobilisation (D'aveni, 1978; Galasckiewicz, 1989), the reproduction of skills (Grieco and Hosking, 1987) and communication effectiveness (Bonacich, 1990). These contacts may also be useful in highly delicate, failure-prone and volatile agreements such as those among colluding oligopolists (Pfeffer and Salancik, 1978).

(2) *Interlocking directorates* are a specific form of social network characterised by communication, joint decision making, formalised linking-pin roles and social control. They tend to be adopted when the relations between the firms incorporate a high level of uncertainty and the exchange of resources cannot be regulated through formal contracts (Pfeffer and Salancik, 1978; Burt, 1979).

(3) *Industrial districts* are another relevant form of social network. They normally tend to be based on relationships between small firms characterised by geographical and cultural proximity (Brusco, 1982; Bellandi, 1986). In addition to these forms, there are other industrial districts in technology-intensive and dynamic industries that are particularly suitable for managing innovation and intensive interdependences of differentiated firms, coordinated by means of intensive processes of information exchange, confrontation and problem solving (Grandori, 1997). Different industrial districts have been developed over time in different countries, like, for example, in Italy, in the Emilia Romagna region, in some parts of France, and in California and Massachusetts.

Another type of social inter-firm relationships is that characterised by a central agent (asymmetric or centralised). These inter-firm relationships are based on vertical interdependencies. The transactions are in some chronological order, thus firms are often linked by contracts, but these contracts only specify the terms of goods and service exchange and not the organisation of the relationship between firms. Therefore, the inter-organisational relationship itself is not formalised into a contract. Some examples of this form are listed as follows:

(1) *Putting-out* is a form of inter-firm network that has re-appeared recently (Kieser, 1993). It includes the transfer of material – over which a focal firm maintains property rights – to other firms that transform them into more final outputs. This agreement normally generates networks that are centralised as happens in the textile clothing industry in which the social interaction and

coordination between partners is normally combined with authority exchanges (Mariotti and Cainarca, 1986; Whitley, 1991).

(2) *Constellations* are informal relationships of firms in a vertical *filière* with a central firm controlling the critical competencies and uncertainties, that is, silk districts coordinated by the firm controlling the final commercial stage (Lorenzoni and Ornati, 1988; Grandori, 1997). Das and Teng (2002) argue that in order to consider a multiple association of firms as a constellation at least three firms should be involved. Gomes-Casseres (1987) explains the diffusion of constellations with the increasing complexity of products and the emergence of the global economy. He suggests that these forms are particularly suitable for contexts in which economies of scale, the establishment of industry standard and the diffusion of new technologies across industries are key dimensions.

(3) *Subcontracting* is an inter-organisational form where a central firm, the main contractor, negotiates the entire job with a client and delegates contractually parts of the work to specialised subcontractors. This form of collaboration is normally common in mature industries such as the construction and the automobile industry (Dioguardi, 1987; Cainarca and Colombo, 1990). Some forms of subcontracting can be included in the category of social networks because they are regulated through social and cultural norms (Dioguardi, 1990). Some others belong to the bureaucratic category because they involve formal contracts that contain specific indication on the selection procedures, control mechanisms and incentive schemes of subcontractors (Grandori and Soda, 1995). Most of the collaborating partners, or subcontractors, are selected through negotiations. In addition, notwithstanding the short-term nature of the contract, strictly connected to the single job, most of the contractors work on stable, long-term basis with the same partners (Eccles, 1981; Sako and Helper, 1998; Ménard, 2004).

Bureaucratic collaboration forms

Bureaucratic collaborative inter-firm relationships are those coordination modes that are formalised in exchange or associational arrangements. The formal agreement includes both the specifications on the organisational relationship between parties and the terms of the exchange. The strength of this form of relationships derives from the legal system which protects the parties' reciprocal rights to compliant behaviour. Two categories of bureaucratic inter-firm relationships can be found in practice, parity based and centralised forms.

Among parity-based forms of inter-organisational relationships it is possible to recall:

(1) *Inter-firm associations,* which are particularly important in this category. Trade associations are used to provide common services to similar firms that are not linked by a high and specific form of interdependence. The same logic lies behind cartels and federations (Provan, 1983; Staber and Aldrich, 1983; Bower and Rhenman, 1985; Staber, 1987). An associational contract comprises the common goals, the advantages of the participants, members' contributions together with communication and decision-making procedures for the management of the association (Grandori, 1997). Trade associations tend to be in place when there is a high probability of government intervention, with the purpose of influencing government legislators to achieve favourable legislation. Firms that take part to these associations expect to achieve economic benefits like, for example, legal assistance, advantageous agreements with suppliers and relevant sources of information (Oliver, 1990).

(2) *Consortia,* which are a more powerful obligational form of bureaucratic inter-firm relationship. They are juridical agreements characterised by the institution of joint responsibility of participants in relation to any third entities that may interact with the consortium, even if the firms do not share either profit or ownership. They allow firms to combine similar or complementary resources and impose selective criteria for their access, in order to maintain high quality and productivity standards on their outputs. Some examples of these forms can be sale or purchasing consortia, such as those for the production and sale of regional cheese or wine. More 'organic' versions of consortia can be found when a certain number of firms group together to solve specific problems or to generate new knowledge, like for example when universities and research laboratories are involved, where different competencies are applied and the exchange of research-related information is intensive (Grandori, 1997; Evan and Olk, 1990). These types of consortia are effective when participants recognise that the results of their cooperation can be considered as public goods and are only marginally hit by competitive forces. The rationale behind their existence seems to be that parties mainly provide information and expertise and freely benefit from developing further their original common stock of knowledge. The organisation of 'research consortia' tend to be adhocratic, clan and peer-group based. Another form of consortia that is more structured, differentiated and integrated is related to the realisation of complex projects, such as the design and construction of industrial plants. In this case, participants are in charge

of developing the different parts, which will be combined in a subsequent moment. The tasks assigned to the parties should be technically separable in order to allow individual rewards to the different firms. This separation is, however, counterbalanced by various forms of interdependencies linked to the realisation of an integrated output characterised by a desired level of quality and timing, managed through programmes and reciprocal adjustments. In any case, given the problems deriving from activating cooperation in innovative activities due to appropriation concerns, public intervention is often necessary to support these types of consortia (Grandori, 1997).

Two common forms of consortia in the Far East are the Japanese *keiretsu* and the South Korean *chaebol*. The first one is represented by 25–50 different industrial firms centred around a large trading company or a bank. These companies are linked by means of interlocking directorates, bank holding of member company stock shares and social connection between senior managers. The agreement is not to sell their holdings. Some examples of this form are related to different families, such as Mitsubishi and Sumitomo. South Korean chaebols are associations of big firms centred around either a bank or a holding company that is normally owned by a founding family. They rely on the government for capital, and are managed by family members. Examples of these forms are represented by Samsung and Daewoo (Lei and Slocum, 1990).

(3) *Partnerships and alliances.* The first ones are links among partners with different levels of formalisation, like for example groups of researchers that collaborate in firms, while maintaining strong contacts with other firms and universities in the biotechnology industry. Another form of partnership is that instituted by professionals of various kind. Partners in this case cooperate to take advantage of a 'brand name' and to coordinate very complex services in contexts where human capital is the key resource and cannot be easily monitored, so that decision making need to be decentralised (Farrell and Scotchmer, 1988; Powell, 1996; Ménard, 2004). The second ones, alliances, are particularly common when the development or transfer of technologies is in place. One example is represented by airlines, which increasingly coordinate their schedules, flights, maintenance, reservation, and in many cases tariffs (Baker et al., 2002; Ménard, 2004). Gulati and Singh (1998), by studying more than a thousand alliances in 20 years, showed the importance of anticipated coordination costs and the role of contractual hazards in the choice of a governance structure in different industries (biopharmaceutical, new-materials and automobile sectors). These conclusions have also been strengthened by other contributions, which showed the relevance

of the institutional environment, particularly the regime of property rights, in the choice between non-equity and equity forms of alliances (Hennart, 1988; Oxley, 1999; Ménard, 2004).

Among centralised forms, the most important ones are:

(1) *Agency networks* defined as a form of external organisation that is often adopted in the distribution of semi-standardised products and services of intermediate complexity (i.e. insurance policies). Contracts that activate this relationship include exclusivity clauses, inspection and control rights, modes of knowledge transfer and participative incentive rules that can realign the objectives of agents with those of the principal firm (Grandori and Soda, 1995).

(2) *Licensing* is a form of market contract that includes numerous organisational clauses, accompanied by extra-contractual organisational relations (Soda, 1992; Grandori and Soda, 1995). It is a form of agreement in which companies do not take an equity position in one another and that has proliferated both in the manufacturing and service firms. In manufacturing industries it is adopted as a means to enter the markets of a new region or country. In many cases, licensing agreements are entered with foreign firms to develop technologies to a fuller extent. Licensees contribute to diffusing the technology faster than could the pioneering firm alone. The objective of impeding other firms in the industry to impose their standards leads to licence innovative technologies early on. In addition, cross-licensing agreements are common in industries where R&D and other fixed costs are particularly high, but where aggressive competition is a necessary ingredient to maintain a substantial level of innovation. The pharmaceutical and chemical industries are particularly suitable for these forms of collaborative relationships. In some service industries, licensing agreements are considered particularly appealing because they establish a quick market presence with relatively little investment, and because they use a fairly standardised market approach to creating and controlling a global image (Lei and Slocum, 1990).

(3) *Franchising* is a juridical arrangement according to which the franchisor and the franchisee agree to commercialise a product or service adopting a brand name developed and owned by the franchisor. Typically, the franchisee complies with the rules established, in terms of product mix, operating procedures, and quality, and the franchisor normally contributes with managerial advice, training, advertising assistance and site selection (Shane, 1996). It aims at guaranteeing a high and standard quality and visibility of

services and goods, which alternatively would be difficult and costly for customers to search for and assess. It contemplates that a focus firm, the franchisor, is responsible for monitoring and making decisions for a high number of associated firms that want to provide homogeneous products and services under a common brand name. Firm ownership remains independent and even if the presence of an agency contract *strictu sensu* is not a necessary condition – for example, the franchisee is intended to act 'in the interest' of the franchisor – the establishment of a central authority is thought to be justified (Williamson, 1985; Grandori, 1997). However, despite this centralisation, common know-how and market specific competencies should be diffused and controlled by peripheral units in order to achieve the advantages of specialisation and local responsiveness, on the one hand, and action coordination and economies of scale on the other (Grandori, 1997). Franchising agreements are often applied to services that are moderately complex. The reason for this is that it is difficult to monitor the quality of services characterised by a high complexity ex-ante. In other words, this form is normally adopted when quality cannot be standardised, but it is particularly relevant and brand specific (Grandori and Soda, 1995).

Franchising agreements produce problems that are common to other forms of arrangements. In fact, the right to use a brand name requires the franchisor's capacity to monitor franchisees, which have strong incentives to behave opportunistically. Agency problems as well as complex issues of governance going beyond incentives arise (Lafontaine and Raynaud, 2002; Ménard, 2004). For this reason, franchising agreements need incentive systems involving a high level of gain sharing, accompanied by a high level of hierarchical supervision. This latter is achieved thanks to standardisation of outputs, formalised procedures, uniform accounting, information systems, training of personnel and standard contracts (Pilotti and Pozzana, 1990; Grandori and Soda, 1995; Ménard, 2004).

Proprietary collaboration forms

Inter-organisational relationships between firms can always been activated through cross-holding of equities and property rights. This holding of equity or rights is normally formalised and fosters cooperation particularly in settings characterised by uncertain conditions and risks of opportunistic behaviour. There are two relevant forms of inter-firm coordination based on property: parity based and centralised.

Parity-based versions are represented by *joint ventures.* This is an equity form of collaboration that has been demonstrated to be particularly effective for governing R&D and innovative initiatives, production in high technology industries or production with a high level of automation and informationally complex and firm-specific activities, but it is also diffused in mature industrial sectors (Mariotti and Migliarese, 1984; Teece, 1986; Beamish, 1988; Killing, 1988; Turati, 1990; Balcet, 1990). From an organisational point of view, joint ventures assume the form of 'team production' where financial resources and technical know-how are combined. One example of this is represented by production joint ventures (i.e. those established in the automotive industry), where these latter resemble the logic of creation of a classical firm, with a hierarchical structuring, aimed at the exploitation of resources and economies of scale and scope. In some other cases, joint ventures take an 'organic' structure, with very little use of hierarchical coordination, aimed at exploring new combinations of resources. In this case, this form of cooperation is characterised by an 'hostage exchange' function played by the proprietary commitments. This function is effective when low appropriation concerns of the collaboration results, low measurability of partners' performances, and highly specific transactions are in place (Williamson, 1983; Hennart, 1988; Grandori, 1997).

Joint ventures may be in some cases difficult to manage, due to poor partner analysis, psychological distance between partners and difficult incentive system design (Gomes-Casseres, 1987; Lyles, 1987). Even if a joint venture needs not to be symmetrical in the strict sense of an equal equity holding, it is fundamentally a symmetric type of inter-firm relationship because even if firms confer assets of different value, outlining asymmetric equity distributions, they exert balanced levels of power (Grandori and Soda, 1995).

The centralised version of proprietary forms includes *capital ventures.* These cannot be considered as a pure form of financing, because they involve an organisational relationship activated between the investor and the partner firm. They are particularly useful for initiatives that need capital to finance relatively risky and innovative undertakings, like for example high-tech or 'advanced' industries, where getting credit by means of traditional channels is difficult. Intensive information about the partner, significant property rights held by the venture capitalist, the design of communication means for joint decision making and managerial know-how exchanges are the typical ingredients of this form, especially in the start-up phases (Robert, 1991).

This review of different forms of arrangements between firms does not pretend to be exhaustive. However, it encompasses the most common modes of inter-firm relationships.

Common regularities among collaborative forms

Despite the diversity of inter-firm relationships described in the previous section, these forms present some empirical regularities that are normally found in practice. Three headlines encapsulate these consistencies: individual autonomy, resource pooling, and contracting (Ménard, 2004).

Individual autonomy

Even if firms that collaborate share a common interest to do business together, they remain residual claimants with full capacity to make autonomous decisions as a last resort and maintain individual sovereignty and distinct property rights. They have to balance the interests of the activities in which they cooperate and those in which they act independently. In addition, independent firms do not guarantee a continuous effort to collaboration and when opportunities emerge and specific investments are moderate, they may migrate towards other forms of collaboration with other partners (Dyer, 1997; Ménard, 2004).

Pooling of resources

Partners linked by cooperation agreements are constantly oriented towards organising activities and making key decisions on investments or specific assets jointly. They, in fact, adopt these solutions because markets are considered inadequate to combine the relevant resources and capabilities (Teece and Pisano, 1994) and hierarchies would stifle flexibility. Inter-firm relationships are the choice in contexts requiring the combination of unique resources and expertise that are developed and nurtured within the environments of multiple specialised firms (Powell, 1990). It is the ability to enable a highly customised and context specific deployment of such resources by multiple firms in exchanges that gives inter-firm relationships their unique character. A good example of pooling resources is the arrangement that exists between car assemblers and their suppliers. Examining, for example, the competitive advantage of Japanese automakers (Dyer, 1996) the central thesis is that it is derived from the customer specific deployment of Japanese suppliers' physical assets, production capacity and product knowledge encouraged by the cooperative supplier relationships. This corroborates the range of evidence that cooperative inter-firm relationships enable the leverage of valuable assets and resources committed to the exchange (Henderson, 1990). One important category of these resources is represented by intangible assets whose role in determining the governance choice of firms has been accentuated in multiple contributions. Studies of decision contexts, as in the aerospace or transportation industries, reveal the specificity of intangible assets in the form of human capital to be the central issue determining the choice of governance form for the activity. Evidence from the semiconductor industry shows that the choice of in-house semiconductor fabrication or outsourced fabrication by semiconductor design firms depends on the level of specific investments in specialised communication codes required to effectively interface the collaborating firms (Monteverde, 1995). The cumulative evidence across these studies strongly suggests that intangible assets are significant in determining the character of inter-firm relationships (Subramani and Henderson, 1999).

Contracting

Inter-firm collaborative relationships are normally regulated by contracts that may present different levels of formalisation. Normally, these contracts include some guidelines and principles on how to regulate and organise transactions and on how to share profit and solve potential appropriation concerns. The problem is that it is not possible to contractually specify every possible contingency involved in managing a cooperative entity. Therefore, the legal agreement must be integrated by 'extra-contractual' and organisational constraints of convention, custom and expedience to regulate collaboration (Ménard, 2004).

To sum up, briefly, collaborative relationships between firms possess characteristics that generate a mix of cooperation (because partners share resources) and autonomy (because they are not able to fully regulate their inter-organisational transactions with a contract and struggle with other firms within or outside their networks). They incorporate a tension between legal independence and business interdependence.

Why firms collaborate

After describing the variety of collaborative forms, this chapter explains the reasons for their activation and the different perspectives that have been developed over time to justify their formation. In addition, the most important determinants and influencing factors for their proliferation are highlighted.

The reasons of collaboration between firms

There are several views regarding why firms collaborate. The common theme underlying these views is that the value that partners gain through synergies exceeds what could have been generated through alternative organisational configurations. Recent analyses suggest that collaboration is one of the most powerful enablers of value creation. Value creation in this context refers to the process by which the capabilities of the partners are combined, so that the competitive advantage of either the network as a whole or the single partners is improved. Inter-organisational relationships contribute to value creation through several sources including scale economies, the effective management of risk, cost-efficient market entities, and learning from partners. Moreover, they help to minimise transaction costs, cope with uncertain environments, provide a way to overcome agency problems, reduce partner dependence on resources outside their control, and successfully reposition themselves in dynamic markets (Spekman et al., 1998; Das and Teng, 2000).

In the following section, the theories of inter-organisational collaborations will be presented.

Theories of collaboration

Research on inter-firm collaboration has posited theories addressing the reasons why firms enter into closer business relationships (Grandori and Soda, 1995; Madhok, 1998; Ireland et al., 2002). The theories considered here are the following: the resource-based view, the transaction cost economics, the agency theory, and the social network theory. Each theory explains why and when it is necessary to form a partnership.

Resource-based view

The resource-based approach deals with the firms' creation, usage, and pursuit of resources and capabilities with sustainable rent-yielding potential, which is the source of a long lasting competitive advantage. Sustainable rents are the result of tacit, organisationally embedded, and socially complex resources and capabilities which cannot be easily replicated by others (Reed and DeFillippi, 1990; Barney, 1991; Peteraf, 1993; Madhok, 1998; Das and Teng, 2000; Ireland et al., 2002). On the basis of these premises, firms would collaborate with other firms to activate optimal resource configurations in which the result deriving from merging their resources is higher than that of all the other possible combinations (Das and Teng, 2000; Ireland et al., 2002). In addition, they would cooperate because alliances can be a risk and uncertainty absorbing mechanism when partners commit to learn to work together as well as to work to learn together when aiming to maximise the value-creating potential of available resources (Inkpen, 2000; Ireland et al., 2002).

The decision of firms to activate a partnership depends on the existence of some conditions. The *first* reason is related to the fact that firms may not possess all the resources and capabilities necessary to earn sustainable rents in a specific area of activities and it is not able to generate it in-house at a reasonable amount of time and cost, relative to more knowledgeable and better positioned competitors. This is because resources are path-dependent, idiosyncratic and specialised to the past experience of a certain firm, and therefore cannot be easily replicated by other firms (Teece et al., 1997; Madhok, 1998). Even if a firm is in a position to generate these resources and capabilities, the activity would not be efficient due to potential diseconomies of scale, scope and time as compared to the firm which developed them in the past (Dierickx and Cool, 1989; Madhok, 1998). The *second* reason may be that markets are not able to organise effectively resources and capabilities (Kogut and Zander, 1992; Teece and Pisano, 1994; Madhok, 1998). This is due to the fact that many sources of competitive advantage are 'rooted in high performance routines operating inside the firm, embedded in the firm's processes, and conditioned by its history' (Teece and Pisano, 1994: 537). As a consequence, such capabilities are, firstly, embedded in organisational routines which determine the pattern and quality of interactions within the firm; and secondly, they have changed over time to be reciprocally adapted in the search for greater efficiency and effectiveness, and are therefore difficult to identify, assess, and trade through market transactions without losing part of their value (Madhok, 1996). Such resources cannot be exchanged on the market because the price mechanism does not allow the coordination of transactions that require intensive and continuous interaction. Therefore, transactions that generate synergies from an integrated bundle of complementary and embedded resources require the flexible and systematic exchange of information that inter-firm relationships are equipped to facilitate (Madhok, 1998). Finally, the *third* reason for partnerships formation is to impede acquisition. This is because acquisition would require the definition of a price for targeted capabilities which are difficult to evaluate because any attempt to separate them from their context to allow their value determination would lead to a corresponding loss of value for them. In order to avoid this risk, activating an alliance may provide a solution (Madhok, 1998).

Transaction cost economics

This organisational economics perspective suggests that the suitable governance structure in a specific context is the one that maximises the level of efficiency in carrying out specific transactions (Williamson, 1985, 1991). Following this logic, inter-firm relationships would be activated when collaborating partners can earn rents that are superior to what could have been generated in the absence of the partnership (Ireland et al., 2002). Therefore, collaboration with partner firms is successful when the firms organise their boundary spanning activities in a way that minimises the combination of production and transaction costs. Therefore, inter-firm alliances emerge as the ability of firms to reduce coordination costs, which result from the decomposition of tasks among partners, and the coordination of activities achieved by means of joint decision-making processes and their corresponding communication modes. (Heide and John, 1990; Parkhe, 1993; Gulati, 1998; Gulati and Singh, 1998; Ireland et al., 2002). Inter-organisational relationships would be preferred when transactions are characterised by an intermediate amount of asset specificity since the characteristics of the collaborating governance structure, like for example the intermediate levels of adaptability to changing circumstances, of incentive intensity in terms of means-ends link, and of administrative control, tend to be more optimally aligned with the transaction characteristics (Madhok, 1998).

Agency theory

Agency theory provides an alternative view to explain the emergence of collaboration arrangements. Under conditions of uncertainty, firms cannot be sure that individuals are operating in the interests of the organisation, without incurring monitoring costs to do so. This incorporates two problems: adverse selection and moral hazard (Jensen and Meckling, 1976). According to the agency perspective, these problems could be solved by activating inter-organisational arrangements, which provide residual claimancy to partner firms (Jensen, 1983). In this way, in fact, the presence of residual claimancy would align the partners' goals with that of the principal firm, reducing in this way potential opportunistic behaviours. These forms would be particularly useful in a context of firm expansion because they would allow firms to increase the level of resource endowment, deterring moral hazard and adverse selection problems at a lesser amount of monitoring efforts (Teece, 1986; Larson, 1992; Shane, 1996).

Social network theory

According to this theory the activation of collaboration with other firms is the result of being part of a social context, made up of the accumulation of prior alliances between firms. These direct and indirect ties generate a social network in which firms are incorporated, and which represents an important source of information on the reliability and capabilities of current and potential collaborating partners. This information contributes to selecting new ties opportunities and increases trust in future collaborators. By representing conduits for information, social networks of previous alliances are an important reference point for deciding future alliance formation (Gulati, 1995). This evolution of alliances make the social network dynamic, so that the position of a firm in the network is not fixed but it is the result of the past and the future alliances activated between the collaborating firms belonging to the same network. Thus, as new ties modify the social network that in turn shapes alliances formation, there is a dynamic interaction between action and structure, which can be understood only if analysed over a sufficient amount of time. In this way, it is possible to grasp the emergent structuration that shapes firms' behaviour (Giddens, 1984). This means that history matters when firms make decisions on whom to collaborate with. According to Penrose (1959) current decisions define a future irreversible path-dependent trajectory. The choices of allies made today can have an impact on tomorrow's partners selection. This historical trend is even more complex because it depends also on collaboration decisions of other firms. Therefore, on the basis of Penrose's perspective the path dependence of alliance decisions is not only based on capabilities but also on structural dimensions. So capabilities-based arguments should be combined with social structural ideas to explain firms' decisions of collaboration (Gulati, 1995).

The determinants of collaboration

One of the most relevant issues in the inter-organisational literature is related to explaining the reasons and preconditions of various forms of collaboration with other firms. *Reasons* are related to the contingencies that lead to the inter-organisational relationships activation. *Preconditions* concerns the environmental and organisational elements that will increase the probability that the inter-organisational relationships emerge. Oliver (1990: 242–248), by integrating the existing literature on the topic, describes six generalisable determinants of relationship formation: necessity, asymmetry, reciprocity, efficiency, stability, and legitimacy. Although each factor can be considered as a sufficient condition for collaborating with a partner firm, these factors may act jointly in the decision to establish an inter-organisational relationship.

Necessity is related to the establishment of linkages or exchanges with other organisations as a result of legal or regulatory requirements. These requirements may derive from various authorities, such as government agencies, legislation, industry or professional regulatory bodies and so on. Different authors have distinguished between voluntary inter-organisational relationships that emerge as structures of mutual adjustment, intermediate forms of alliance structures and mandated corporate structure of coordination (Warren, 1967; Whetten, 1981). In those situations where inter-organisational relationships are the result of an imposition from higher authorities, the implications of non-compliance, like for example no access to specific resources or exclusion from the field will increase the probability of mandated associations to occur. The distinction between mandated versus voluntary inter-organisational relationships is particularly relevant because both the determinants and the implications are fundamentally different. The remaining conditions that are described in the following are related to voluntary interactions.

Asymmetry is a contingent variable that describes inter-organisational relationships formation as an attempt to exercise power or control over another organisation or its resources. This perspective suggests that resource scarcity prompts organisations to attempt to exercise power, influence or control over entities that are endowed with the necessary limited resources. In addition, the contention that organisational efforts to control interdependence explains relationships formation is strengthened by the argument that relationships formation requires the loss of decision-making discretion, an implication that most organisations would like to avoid. Therefore, both the attempt to control, and the reluctance to give up control represent asymmetric reasons in the decision to interact. Different theories of political economy (Zeitz, 1980), resource dependence (Pfeffer and Salancik, 1978), class hegemony and elitism (Palmer, 1983) and financial control (Kotz, 1978) link the establishment of inter-organisational relationships to motives of power and control. The environments in which organisations operate are considered as political or negotiated contexts in which injustice, information distortion, manipulation, exploitation, coercion, inequality or conflict prevail (Cook, 1977; Pfeffer and Salancik, 1978; Whetten, 1978; Zeitz, 1980). In this respect, collaboration with other firms is a means to overcome some of these problems. Most of the studies have not tested power as a motive in inter-organisational arrangements' formation.

Another important determinant of collaborative inter-organisational relationships formation is represented by *reciprocity*. This condition refers to cooperation, and coordination among partners. Inter-organisational relationships are activated because partners see opportunities for pursuing common or mutually beneficial objectives more than for exerting domination, power and control. Motives of reciprocity emphasise collaboration between organisations, rather than domination, power and control. This factor may also contribute to explaining the development of certain inter-organisational relationships that would be difficult to explain otherwise. For example, an association between two joint venture partners that want to pursue new markets or activities represents a direct alternative to the resource dependence perspective. A reciprocity model on inter-firm agreements is theoretically consistent with exchange theory (Emerson, 1962), the finance capital theory of inter-corporate relations (Scott, 1985), the reciprocity model of director interlocks (Koenig et al., 1979) and the collective strategy framework (Oliver, 1988). This model is based on a certain number of assumptions: first, resources scarcity may lead to cooperation instead of competition (Schermerhorn, 1981); second, the formation of the relationships is characterised by mutual support, collaboration rather than domination and conflict; finally, the partners realise that the participation in the relationship generates more advantages than disadvantages, specifically the loss of decision-making discretion and the cost of managing the relationship (Provan, 1984).

Efficiency is a determinant factor that is linked to the attempt to maximise the internal input/output ratio, rather than the need to comply with higher authorities' requirements, the wish to exert power and control over another entity, or the will to achieve joint inter-organisational objectives. The purpose is to increase return on assets, reduce unit costs, waste, downtime or cost per client. This logic is consistent with transaction cost economics, according to which transaction cost economisation determines whether activities will be carried out in market, hierarchies, or inter-organisational governance forms (Williamson, 1985). When these latter form may reduce transaction costs, as a result of higher asset specificity (the existence of significant and redeployable investments), high uncertainty and a high frequency of transactions, the probability of abandoning pure market forms, for more intermediate structures increases.

Economic theories that concentrate on efficiency as a criterion for explaining governance forms, yet, have focussed more on the consequences of inter-organisational relationships more than their determinants. More specifically, they have focussed on the negative impact that inter-organisational relationships may have on the market, such as the effect of inter-organisational coordination on restricting competition (Gupta and Lad, 1983), the economic stagnation (Olson, 1982), the impact of social structures on impeding market rivalry (Granovetter, 1985).

An additional critical factor of relationships formation is *stability* (predictability). On the basis of this perspective the activation of collaborative relationships is an adaptive response to environmental uncertainty, deriving from resource scarcity, lack of perfect knowledge about fluctuations, availability of exchange partners, and available rates of exchange in inter-firm field (Thompson, 1967; Cook, 1977; Pennings, 1981; Williamson, 1985). This uncertainty pushes organisations to activate relationships in order to increase stability and predictability. Inter-organisational relationships serve as strategies to absorb uncertainty and increase forecasting capabilities in order to achieve an orderly and reliable pattern of resource flows and exchanges (Pennings, 1981). Several empirical studies have investigated the role of inter-firm associations in achieving this purpose (i.e Provan, 1984; Stearns et al., 1987).

Finally, *legitimacy* has also been addressed as an important determinant of inter-firm relationships formation (Meyer and Rowan, 1977; Zucker, 1977; DiMaggio, 1988). According to the neo-institutional theory organisations try to be isomorphic to the environment because they receive pressures from institutions, represented by norms, rules, beliefs or expectations of external constituents. Given these premises collaborative relationships between firms are activated with the objective of increasing legitimacy in terms of reputation, image, prestige or congruence with prevailing norms in its institutional environment. The target partner may be represented by other member's of the organisation's set, licensing boards, resource-granting agencies, the general public, external stakeholders and, in general, any entity whose level of legitimacy is perceived to be higher than its own (Galaskiewicz, 1985). Contributions that have empirically investigated the role of legitimacy are, however, only a few. For example, Wiewel and Hunter (1985) showed that new organisations increased their legitimacy thanks to their ability to invoke affiliations with very well-known organisations.

Although each determinant can act as an individual motivation for relationships formation, the decision to activate an collaborative association with partner firms is based on a multiplicity of reasons. For example, complying with legal or regulatory requirements may be reinforced by other expectations such as more power, greater mutual advantage, higher efficiency, greater stability or legitimacy. The determinants of asymmetry and reciprocity may combine for the objective of exerting power over a third organisation. Efficiency may interact with stability or reciprocity. In order to increase efficiency, an entity may pursue stable relationships, expecting that stability will contribute to acquiring additional resources. Similarly, the attempt to pursue mutually beneficial relations may be higher when an organisation expects more internal efficiency from the activation of the relationship. Finally, the interaction between asymmetry and efficiency, and that between asymmetry and stability are more ambiguous and have been only partially dealt with in the literature (Oliver, 1990).

The influencing factors on collaboration proliferation

There are different factors that influence the proliferation of partnerships between firms (Powell, 1987: 77–82). They are related to the quick structural change in the world economy, characterised by a movement of firms away from some specific industries towards a new set of industries and to the emergence of new markets and technologies. Partnerships seem to be suitable organisational forms consistent with these new trends. The organisational elements that seem to count more on the diffusion of collaboration arrangements refer to: high competition and the need for flexibility; differentiated customers' tastes and customization; shorter life-cycles and quick time to market; and the importance of reputation.

High competition and need for flexibility

Big and hierarchical companies operate normally in environments that are not characterised by strong competition. They are capable of achieving economies of scale and tend to be adopted in concentrated industries such as auto and steel industries – especially before the exposure to foreign rivalry – and in the public and non-profit sectors. These organisations are particularly appreciated for their reliability and accountability. Yet, when these organisations start to face unexpected fluctuations in demand and unanticipated changes, the liabilities of large scale are exposed. Problems of structural inertia, risk-aversion, and decreased employee satisfaction and commitment begin to emerge. There is a strong trend towards growth beyond the optimal size and resistance to change. Size leads to more rules and more documentation. Risk-aversion and lack of speed in processing information and in making decisions generates sluggishness. Thus, in settings based on high competitive pressures (as is the case, for example, of semiconductors or biotechnology industries), where rivalry is particularly fierce and leads to a high mortality of organisations, the capability to respond promptly to customers' requests and needs can be better guaranteed by smaller, flatter or leaner enterprises. However, not necessarily these organisations outperform the bigger ones. This is because, although small organisations can adapt their internal structures more quickly to external changes, an organisation under-going change is more vulnerable to environmental shocks. Therefore, the collaboration between small and large firms or the downsizing of larger firms into smaller autonomous work units that cooperate may be considered as a means to overcome inertia, on the one side, and fill the void of legitimacy that plagues small firms on the other. In sum, firms tend to aggregate and collaborate to survive to strong competitive forces (Powell, 1987).

Differentiated customers' tastes and customization

Recently, there has been a radical change towards diversified consumer tastes and customization. Piore and Sabel (1984) suggest that the decline of the mass market for standardised products has produced a decrease in productivity and a slower growth, thus contributing to the emergence of new organisational forms that are more flexible and dynamic, and so more suitable for adapting to these new environmental conditions. What has led the increasing diversity of customer tastes has not been clarified yet. This change has been considered as a reflection of cost reduction in the craft production. This cost reduction is the result in many respects of the diffusion of business skills to a higher number of firms, combined with the diffusion of microcomputer technology and small business software applications.

Regardless of the reasons, however, the emergence of more flexible forms of production, more focus on innovation, and more specialised, higher quality product lines is definitely relevant. Dealing with these new trends requires increased technological sophistication and quicker response time on the part of organisations. These new aspects have led to the downsizing of large integrated firms and the increase of smaller specialised organisations that cooperate, and new hybrid forms. These trends are observed more intensively in mature mass production industries and in traditional sectors where craft production has never been replaced, and in the new high technology industries (Powell, 1987).

Shorter life-cycles and quick time to market

In recent years, as product life cycles have shortened, timing considerations and access to know-how have become relevant problems. In many technologically driven industries, knowing how to manufacture a product and how to make it function properly in a timely manner is a key success factor. Teece and Pisano (1994) argue that the most successful research centres are located outside the boundaries of the large corporation. Whether one firm's technological know-how has prevailed, or innovations are difficult to replicate internally, there is an increasing need to get access to technological innovation quickly. Partnerships or coalitions are an effective way of regaining success and are less costly, less irreversible, and more feasible than internal solutions.

In addition, often knowledge to innovate is tacit and is difficult to formalise; therefore, it cannot be easily communicated and diffused. In this context, specialised knowledge that has been developed and accumulated over time cannot be easily appropriated and cannot be found in formal documents such as manuals or handbooks. Inter-organisational forms represent a fast mode of getting access to new knowledge outside the organisation, without bearing the risk that this knowledge will easily become outdated. This is because inter-firm arrangements maintain some degree of independence and so the costs of investing in new knowledge is shared among the partners autonomously. They generate multiple networks of communication, contributing in this way to furthering innovation by integrating different perspectives and knowledge repositories (Powell, 1987).

Importance of reputation

In many aspects, inter-firm collaborating forms re-propose a traditional method for resource allocation, according to which transactions do not take place by means of discrete exchanges and administrative mechanisms, but through networks of subjects that are involved in reciprocal, preferential, mutually supportive actions. In this type of relationships reputation, image and trust and the lack of a calculative logic guide the system of exchanges. Single units exist not by themselves, but in relationship to other units. One of the main tenet of this network logic is the adoption of a long-term perspective. Stability and longevity lead to the exploration of more effective and efficient way for achieving results. When transactions occur in a certain volume and with a certain frequency the focus moves away from quantity and shifts to quality. The reputation of a partner becomes the most explicit sign of its reliability. Reputation is so important because in these types of relationships the distinction between formal business and social roles is really blurred. As a consequence, hierarchical supervision plays only a marginal role, because involvement in the network prevents free-riding. Self-monitoring and peers assessment become the suitable mechanisms of governance. Performance evaluation is not based on explicit indicators but on soft signals sent by those that work together (Ouchi, 1979).

Networked forms of organisation are particularly suitable for those contexts where efficient and reliable information is necessary. The relevant information is not that passing through formal communication channels or that can be implicitly assumed by analysing prices. As Kaneko and Imai (1987) suggest information passed through networks is 'thicker' than information obtained in the market, and 'freer' than that communicated in a hierarchy. According to this logic, collaboration between firms in a network is the preferred form, where partners base their exchanges on social connections (Powell, 1987).

How to organise firms' collaboration

After illustrating the variety and the reasons for collaboration between firms, this chapter aims at furthering our understanding by describing how the underlying interaction is organised. The recognition of the hybrid nature of these organisational forms is another fundamental step towards the clarification of their control peculiarities.

How to choose governance structures to organise business exchanges

The growing importance of inter-firm relationships in the last decades has motivated a rethinking of the logic of economic organisation, that is, the existence of firms and the determinants of the choice between hierarchical governance, market governance and hybrid governance. In fact, the organisation of economic activities in practice appear to be increasingly moving away from the pure models of 'markets' and 'firms' towards 'hybrid' models. These latter form a specific class of governance structures and are instantiated in a variety of cooperative inter-firm arrangements (see Chapter 1) that execute a broad range of activities that were previously completely carried out within organisations or through market exchanges.

Notwithstanding the impressive set of organisational studies on hybrids referenced so far, this terrain is still a shifting one and the vocabulary is not well stabilised. Indeed, there is a sense of common knowledge regarding the concepts of both market, centred on the mechanics of supply and demand and on the role of prices as key to its functioning, and firms, with the importance of hierarchical authority in sustaining activities and decision-making processes. On the contrary, the set of arrangements that rely neither solely on prices nor on authority for organising transactions is broad and potentially confusing (Ménard, 2004).

Before proceeding to characterise inter-firm relationships as hybrid governance structures, it is important to define the concept of *governance structure*.

Such notion is key to *transaction cost economics (TCE)*. Although TCE is a detailed and sophisticated theoretical framework, rooted in neo-classical economics, it raises many of the central issues that face managers within organisations as it represents the most elaborate attempt to explain to what extent firms may decide to integrate their operations (Bradach and Eccles, 1989). This theoretical framework draws on the work of Commons (1934), who suggested that the transaction should be viewed as the basic unit of analysis of economic activity.

Coase (1937) emphasised that transactions may be organised through a market or within a firm. Each of these structures displays specific functioning costs. Nearly 40 years later, Arrow and Williamson developed some of these arguments: Arrow (1974) suggested that firms and markets are alternative means to organise economic activity while Williamson (1975, 1985, 1991) analysed governance structures in a comparative institutional way. He specifically defined governance structure as 'the explicit or implicit contractual framework within which a transaction is located' (Williamson, 1981: 1544) as well as a means to infuse order in a relation where potential conflicts may prevent counterparts to realise mutual gains.

TCE is mostly associated with the work of this last author. One reason why Williamson's contribution is so significant is that it represents one of the first and most important efforts to develop an economic theory whose aim is to explain the structure of firms, while previous economic theories treated the firms as 'black boxes'. In particular, Williamson's importance lies in specifying the variables that determine whether the 'market' or the 'firm' will be used to organise and manage business transactions in various circumstances depending on the characteristics of the transactions themselves. The least costly, that is, the most efficient, governance structure will be the one chosen to organise business transactions. According to Williamson (1975, 1981, 1985), one of the most important features of a governance structure lies in its ability to *economise on transaction costs*, that is, the costs of making an exchange. By identifying and evaluating transaction costs it is possible to compare different governance structures and choose the most efficient one.

The underpinnings of his framework are *two behavioural assumptions*: opportunism and bounded rationality.

(1) *Opportunism*: refers to the fact that people will possibly act in a self-interested way and may not be honest about their intentions. They even might profit of unforeseen situations to exploit their counterparts and decide to bar themselves to disclose all relevant information for the transaction at their own advantage. According to TCE not all people will act opportunistically all of the time but one needs to assume that some people may act opportunistically some of the time, and it is impossible to tell in advance whether a specific person is an opportunist.

(2) *Bounded rationality* is related to the limited cognitive processing power and limited memories of individuals who can, by nature, neither

absorb all the relevant information nor elaborate all the consequences and the possible alternative courses of action related to the information they possess. Bounded rationality points to the fact that decision makers need to recognise the limitations both of the information available to them and their ability to handle its complexity. This is partly because reaching a decision itself is inherently too complex (there are too many alternatives), and also because the actions of the other parties involved are unpredictable.

These assumptions represent an innovation with respect to standard economic models, but not a radical one. In fact, individuals are self-interested, though opportunistic behaviour is not expected by definition. Likewise, similarly to traditional economic theory, individuals are viewed as rational, that is, as profit maximisers, but according to TCE there are some limitations they need to take into account to their capacity to make a rational decision to accomplish this end.

The practical lesson to be learned from these assumptions is that it is necessary to 'organise transactions so as to economise on bounded rationality while simultaneously safeguarding them against the hazards of opportunism' (Williamson, 1996: 254).

Starting from these premises, Williamson's main argument is that one of the most important features of a governance structure is its capacity to economise on transaction costs and that by assessing transaction costs it is possible to evaluate different governance structures. Being a transaction cost a cost incurred in making an economic exchange, its determinants are related to the characteristics of business exchanges, that is, of transactions. These latter can be frequent or rare; have high or low uncertainty; or involve specific or non-specific assets. Frequency, uncertainty and asset specificity thus determine decisions about which governance structure to use, that is, more practically said, whether to integrate vertically.

In particular:

(1) *Frequency*: no firm would want to bring 'in-house' the provision of a good or service that is very rarely used. For example, most firms will not want to set up their own management consultancy departments because they only use the services of a management consultant on a very infrequent basis. Of course, if firms use consultants frequently, they may decide to set up an in-house operation.

31

(2) *Uncertainty*: it is related to how difficult it is to predict the possible events that might happen during the course of the transaction. It implies incomplete information, that is, some of all the relevant information to the problem is missing. Uncertainty is also linked to the duration of the transaction. For transactions that take place on markets one has to cope with relatively little uncertainty, because they are spot ones, while transactions needing a commitment over time have some uncertainty natively embedded in them. The neo-classical market is instantaneous, and has neither past nor future. For this reason, in the market, the existence of long-term and personal relationships, and of trust is impossible. Coase (1937) maintains that a firm is likely to come out in those situations where short-term contracts would be inadequate and that 'it seems improbable that a firm would emerge without the existence of uncertainty.' As an example, let us consider a supplier of a specific car component agreeing to provide it to an auto maker. Both counterparts would like a reasonably long-term agreement to enable them to plan their respective activities. However, the long-term nature of the relationship increases uncertainty: how can the component supplier be confident that the auto maker will not fail during the contract, thereby putting at risk its own business? Such uncertainty would be problematic also because of: bounded rationality – it is impossible to foresee all the possible occurrences impacting on the relationship; information asymmetries – the supplier does not know everything about the financial and competitive position of the auto maker; and opportunism – is the supplier sure that the information disclosed to her or him by the buyer are correct and vice versa?

(3) *Asset specificity* refers to transactions requiring assets that are idiosyncratic, that is, only valuable if employed to sustain a specific business relationship. In the case of buyer–supplier relationships, the problems arise if specific assets are owned by both, since this will probably result in prolonged and complex negotiation on the division of profits from business exchanges. This originates a situation in which both parties are *'locked-in' the relationship* as, with asset specificity, large-numbers bargaining is transformed into small-number bargaining. Moreover, whenever a buyer requires a particular investment from a supplier which would be advantageous for both there can be a risk for the latter. In fact, after the investment has been made, it becomes a sunk cost and the buyer can attempt to re-negotiate the contract at his own advantage. This is the so-called hold-up *problem*,

which arises when either party asymmetrically sustains significant costs or benefits before being paid for or paying for them.

Six types of asset specificities may be outlined:

(a) physical specificity (e.g. specialised equipment or infrastructures to serve some particular relationship);

(b) dedicated assets (e.g. high-capacity equipment dedicated to a particular buyer);

(c) human asset specificity (e.g. specialised knowledge and procedures to interact with a counterpart);

(d) brand-name capital (e.g. brand names which imply high quality or other distinctive product/service features);

(e) temporal specificity (e.g. timing of delivery or production);

(f) site specificity (e.g. geographic proximity to resources or suppliers).

Simply put, *as the levels of frequency, uncertainty and asset specificity increase, business transactions become more likely to be vertically integrated* and governed using hierarchical rather than market governance mechanisms. More precisely, which governance structure should be employed to regulate transactions depends on the aforementioned transaction attributes, with the latter having a crucial role. In fact, as asset specificity increases, the least costly governance structure varies, in a discrete manner, from markets to hierarchical governance.

Why choosing between market and hierarchy when you can use both? The 'hybrid' alternative

The emphasis of TCE has always been – at least till the first half of the 1990s – on the trade-off between markets and firms. The make-or-buy logics is an exemplification of the main assumption of the transaction cost approach, that is, that markets and firms are mutually exclusive means for allocating resources (Bradach and Eccles, 1989).

The core of *markets* is represented by supply and demand and by the prices as adaptation mechanisms which perform three main tasks (Hennart, 1993):

(1) inform parties,

(2) rule bargaining,

(3) provide rewards and punishments.

The information structure of markets is decentralised: each counterpart receives all information through prices – which are exogenous – and adapts to it in a way that maximises joint welfare.

The neo-classical theory sustains that market exchanges between rational counterparts, concerned in maximising their own value, will lead to an equilibrium between supply and demand among all market participants. More specifically, the ideal notion of market rests on three assumptions:

(1)   individuals have rational preferences among outcomes that are associated with a value;
(2)   individuals aims at maximising their utilities (i.e. their well being depending both on their welfare and their preferences) and firms aims at maximising profits;
(3)   individuals take action independently on the basis of full and relevant information, that is to say on prices.

Markets' functioning relies on classical contract law, according to which the identities of the counterparts are irrelevant and reciprocal dependence is insignificant. As a result, parties on the market should behave in strict adherence to contractual terms. If not, courts are appealed to regulate and solve disputes. Besides, price is the main means of communication and counterparts are motivated by competition incentive, while control intensity is weak.

The idea of pure market was firstly discussed and questioned by Coase in his two renowned papers, 'The nature of the firm' (1937) and 'The problem of social cost' (Coase, 1960). The author maintained that if all the assumptions of classical economics became real in practice, the world would resemble Adam Smith's ideal market of small producers engaging in optimal, wealth-maximising exchanges. Nevertheless, these assumptions are not entirely realised: in 'The nature of the firm', in fact, Coase asked himself why large business organisations, which do not exist in Adam Smith's world, exist in real world and answered that they exist since real-life market exchanges are not costless. Thus, *firms* will develop until the costs of organising economic activities within themselves stand below the costs of organising economic activity through the market.

Firms rely on hierarchical authority. Within firm, routines and hierarchical structures ensure communication between individuals (March and Simon, 1958), who are disciplined and controlled by means of behavioural constraints.

Information is centralised as individuals are asked to report information to a central party who incorporates it and give it back to others in the form of directives. Administrative controls within firms give greater power to monitor and discipline individuals than a market permits (Powell, 1990). Besides, firms are founded on the forbearance principle as stated by Williamson, who maintained that 'hierarchy is its own ultimate court of appeal' (Williamson, 1996: 98). The parties in a dispute resolve their differences internally, drawing on *fiat* that cannot be exercised in market. However, incentives (career, status, salary) within firms are weaker than in markets.

According to TCE, therefore, one should choose in a *mutually exclusive way either to buy externally (the market) or to integrate vertically (the firm)* contingent on the relative costs of the two options which, in turn, depend on the characteristics of the transaction and of the exchange context (see Table 3.1).

However, there is one major problem with this reasoning. Elements of these two ideal types are often found mixed together in the real world as exemplified by Powell (1990):

- Craft work – like in the construction, publishing and film and recording industries – is project based. In publishing firms, bureaucracy is used the least possible and they count on the editor's network of personal relations. In film and recording industries boundaries are blurred, work roles are quite fuzzy and responsibilities overlapping, and work ties cross teams and other organisations;
- Industrial districts, like in Italy (Modena), where firms are small, with little vertical integration and all located in an industrial region. Among these firms there are collaborative subcontracting agreements. In districts, trust and mutual dependency facilitate the flow of information among the partners and spatial concentration implies the proximity to skilled people, the cooperation of local government, easier and stronger ties to research institutes and trade associations;
- Strategic partnerships in research and development which allow faster access to new technologies, economies of scale in joint research and/or production, share the risks for activities and broader sources of know-how.

Starting from observation of reality, as explained in the following sections, also literature has begun to study and norm that myriad of organisational forms existing along with markets and pure firms that get instantiated in stable long-term relationships between independent exchange partners.

Table 3.1   A comparison of the two pure forms: market vs firm.

	Market	Firm
Conditions under which transactions costs are minimised by each governance structure	• Markets are made of 'large numbers' and there is no asset specificity • Buyer and seller relationships are short term and infrequent. Transactions are instantaneous • Uncertainty is low (few and known contingencies) • There is symmetric information • The counterparts' identity is irrelevant • The object of the transaction is represented by standardised goods or services	• There is high asset specificity • Counterparts transact frequently • Uncertainty is often high (too many and too complex contingencies) • There is asymmetric information • Identity of the parties involved in the transaction matters • The object of the transaction is represented by customised and/or complex goods and services
Transaction costs	*Coordination costs*: • Slight search cost • Slight cost of monitoring • Slight cost of litigation (legal actions are not likely, but when they happen they are regulated by means of courts) *Motivation costs:* • High cost of cheating	*Coordination costs*: • High cost of administrating • High cost of monitoring • High cost for processing information *Motivation costs*: • High cost of shirking
How coordination is reached	• The contract specifics • The court	• Mutual adjustment • Direct work supervision • Standardisation of outputs • Standardisation of processes • Standardisation of inputs
How motivation is reached	• *Rewards*: Surplus from the exchange. For the buyer, it is the value he or she attaches to the good or service he or she receives less the price paid. For the seller, it is the price he or she receives less the value he or she attaches to the good or service he or she provides (e.g. total cost of producing and delivering it). • *Sanctions*: To buy or sell from another counterpart	• *Rewards*: For the employer, it is the value of the labour services. For the employee, it is the salary plus the bonuses, and any other fringe benefit. • *Sanctions*: It is mainly a problem of the employee who can get fired or get reduction in his or her salary and fringe benefits
Efficiency	Potentially short run efficient	Potentially long run efficient

Recently, the conceptual apparatus of TCE theory has been extended to recognise the existence of a third governance form termed 'hybrid' (Williamson, 1994). As the name suggests, this generic governance alternative incorporates certain attributes of both markets and hierarchical organisations, but blends them to generate a unique exchange environment, distinct from those observed in markets and firms (Williamson, 1994). Following this line of reasoning, some recent works have described economic exchanges that present more and more a mix of both market-like and hierarchical features thus overcoming the traditional trade-off between market and firms, incorporated in the make-or-buy logics. Such contributions (Holland and Lockett, 1997; Zenger and Hesterly, 1997; Tomkins, 2001; Amigoni et al., 2003) have demonstrated the existence of hybrid structures as a feasible alternative to the two pure forms of markets and hierarchies, arguing that in such mixed-mode operations the distinction between elements of both market and hierarchy is one of degree.

One key critique that these recent contributions have made to TCE is that it is necessary to distinguish between *organising methods* (*hierarchy* and the *price system*) and *institutions* (*markets* and *firms*). Even though firms rely mainly on hierarchy and markets on prices, each one of these economic institutions may use one or both organising methods, each one having its costs and benefits given the specific circumstances. In this respect, it is important to know that:

(1) prices reward individuals on the basis of their outputs while hierarchy on the basis of their behaviours;
(2) the costs of using prices are the cheating costs, that is, the cost of measuring outputs together with the losses due to fraud when such measurement is not perfect;
(3) the costs of using hierarchy are the shirking costs, that is, the cost related to the use of behaviour constraints plus the costs due to imperfect behaviour constraints;
(4) price constraints minimise shirking but encourage cheating;
(5) hierarchical constraints minimise cheating but encourage shirking.

Therefore, any business exchange will be organised by that specific mix of organising methods that minimise costs. Such mix defines a wide variety of institutional forms lying in the spectrum spanned by markets and firms at polar end-points. Those economic institutions are mixed-mode forms and for this reason they are called *hybrids*, to differentiate them from the pure spot markets and traditional firms (Hennart, 1993: 531–32).

The distinguishing features and the management mechanisms of hybrids

Not only has a growing body of literature established the idea that hybrids are often more efficient of both markets and firms, but also practice has showed that they are becoming established as a model for success (Ménard, 2004). In fact, although these organisational forms arise for many reasons, a generic goal of hybrids is to avoid the disadvantages of conventional, unitary organisations. These latter, among other things, often suffer from operational inefficiency, resource scarcity, lack of facilities to take advantage of economies of scale, and risks that would be more appropriately spread across several business partners. Hybrids offer a wide range of solutions to such problems because they draw upon the capabilities of multiple, independent organisations as they are organisational arrangements that use resources and or governance structures from more than one single firm, encompassing a broad range of organisational combinations (Borys and Jemison, 1989).

The blooming literature on hybrid arrangements provides a clear indication of the growing interest for the multiple issues they arise (Ménard, 2004). The perspectives in such literature reflect the concerns of several disciplines that have aimed at examining the phenomenon. For instance, the competitive implication of inclusion and exclusion of firms in hybrids receives considerable attention in the *strategy* literature (Gomes-Casseres, 1994), while the nature and role of contracts in cooperative arrangements is the focus of the *legal* perspective (Palay, 1984). The role of trust and reciprocal norms in the organisation of collaboration relationships is central to the *organisational* literature (Ring and Van de Ven, 1992, 1994; Zaheer and Venkatraman, 1995; Grandori and Soda, 1995) while the enabling role of information technologies is central to the examinations of hybrid governance in the *information system* literature (Zaheer and Venkatraman, 1994). A *finance*-based analysis focuses on how hybrids make possible potential gains from increased access to capital and diversification. Further, the control mechanisms and the role of management accounting in supporting inter-firm relations in a supply chain are central to a growing body of *management accounting* literature on hybrids (e.g. Cooper and Slagmulder, 1999; Berry, 2000).

More generally speaking, there are some distinguishing features of hybrid organisational forms both on the formal and on the informal levels.

From the *formal* point of view, hybrids rely on *contracts*. The major advantage of such mechanism is its generalisability throughout the economy, which implies that the contract is the mechanism most easily available and potentially understandable to different hybrid partners. On the contrary, its main disadvantage is related to the well-known trade-off between flexibility and richness, which correspondingly lead to the problems of opportunism and information asymmetries (Ouchi, 1978; Granovetter, 1985; Williamson, 1985; Lorenz, 1988) that are demonstrated to be particularly severe in hybrid settings (Holland and Lockett, 1997; Zenger and Hesterly, 1997). More specifically, hybrids rely on neo-classical, relational contracts, in which the identity of exchanging partners is central. Thanks to these contracts, as explained by Stinchcombe (1985) and Bradach and Eccles (1989), a lot of features of hierarchical firms are routinely obtained in inter-firm agreements. The idea that authority can be achieved by other means than hierarchical governance, like contractual provisions, is central to the analysis of hybrid governance tools.

Ex-post governance mechanisms are also necessary in the management of hybrids to fill the gap of contract incompleteness. The following are the most common authority mechanisms that are used in hybrids. These can be also written into contracts:

(1) inspection arrangements,
(2) quality control systems,
(3) methods for adjusting prices, costs, quantities and times,
(4) incentive systems based on performance,
(5) agreements about the allocation of decision rights and about who has to the authority to modify contractual provisions,
(6) rules and standard operating procedures (that create expectations of continuity and dependability),
(7) standard practices which tie each partner's operations to the overall functioning of the hybrid.

Yet, it is important to underline that with respect to the recourse to hierarchical mechanisms, there are relevant differences between hybrids and unitary organisations. In fact, while such mechanisms are based on authority that is taken for granted in traditional organisations, in hybrids, it is not possible to capitalise on reservoirs of authority, being each partner a sovereign organisation. In effect, goal consensus is indicated as crucial with respect to hybrids' stability: '(...) harmony and conflict resolution are difficult to achieve because partners often do not share a common environment or domain and, thus, lack a foundation for generating a set of common understandings about the purpose of the hybrid and the process by which that purpose can be achieved' (Borys and Jemison, 1989: 237). Similarly, Scott (1987) as well underlined that a 'common purpose' is fundamental to grant hybrids' smooth functioning while providing clear direction that acts as a unifying incentive. In this respect, the breadth of the purpose may lead to an important trade-off regarding the hybrid's stability: on the one hand, a broad purpose may represent an adequate stabiliser in the presence of conflicts over narrow interests but, at the same time, in the long run, it may not provide sufficient elements to arbitrate among the specific interests of partners and settle the conflicts down; on the other hand, a narrow purpose certainly allows partners to be unequivocal about reciprocal expectations but it may leave un-addressed many important collateral issues that may threaten the hybrid stability (Borys and Jemison, 1989).

For this reason, hybrids are also characterised by the fact of leveraging on informal mechanisms that maintain a continuity of interaction over multiple contracting periods. From the *informal* point of view, hybrids, in fact, distinguish themselves for the importance of interpersonal relationships and *norms of reciprocity* concerning a vast array of stakes that go well beyond those of purely economic transactions (Uzzi, 1996). In hybrid exchanges, partners may have overlapping roles and incorporate joint activities that require their *ongoing negotiation* and modification in response to specific circumstances as they arise. Hybrids' competitive advantage lies in their considerable flexibility in operations: temporary inequities, such as asymmetric investments, among counterparts can be sustained in the short run as overall equitable outcomes are mutually ensured over multiple periods of interactions (Subramani and Henderson, 1999). Hybrids' counterparts communicate through *relational ties*. The hybrid usually involves firms working together closely, each providing unique capabilities and resources and jointly deriving advantages that neither party could derive on their own. Over multiple periods of relations, relatively stable patterns of interaction between these independent firms are aimed at providing significant benefits to all the participants (Nohria and Eccles, 1992).

An alternative review of the mechanisms that are typically used by hybrids is the one proposed by Grandori and Soda (1995). Though the authors do not provide novel categories for classifying the variety of these mechanisms, their contribution is useful in that it presents a quite comprehensive view on the topic. According to them, the most common studied management mechanisms of hybrids are:

- *Communication, decision and negotiation mechanisms*: being the less costly coordination mechanisms, they are present, with different intensity degrees, in all kinds of hybrids, usually in the form of cross-firm interpersonal networks for sustaining information exchanges and promoting continuous contacts (Aldrich and Whetten, 1981; Granovetter, 1985);

- *Social coordination and control mechanisms*: they are identified as group norms, reputation and peer control (Ouchi, 1978, 1980); their role is said to be fundamental since any kind of stable cooperation relationship has a 'social side' (Griesinger, 1990);
- *Integration and linking-pin roles and units*: these mechanisms are based on the definition of horizontal roles and responsibilities as means for promoting goal congruence in hybrid forms;
- *Common staff*: when activities become significant in number and scope, a dedicated staff may be necessary for granting the functioning of an inter-firm agreement. A positive correlation has been pointed out by empirical evidence between the amount of affiliated firms and the size of central coordination structure. Franchising agreements, joint ventures and consortia are hybrid forms usually characterised by the presence of a central coordination staff;
- *Selection systems*: the specificity of access to a certain inter-organisational arrangement is a very powerful mechanism for enhancing the likelihood of achieving a stable functioning. The selection mechanisms are very important especially in informal socio-cultural hybrids, based on socialisation and shared values (Ouchi, 1980);
- *Incentive systems*: their use is central in a wide range of circumstances in which performance is difficult to measure. In informationally complex activity contexts, profit-sharing and income-sharing systems are widely used: examples can be found in some consortia, in franchising forms and in some associational forms (Daems, 1983). A particularly effective incentive mechanism is that of property rights: joint ventures, equity alliances and consortia for the joint ownership of assets use proprietary commitments and a priori specification of property rights for the 'fair division' of benefits in order to grant their survival/success (Williamson, 1981, 1985);
- *Public support and infrastructures*: when cooperation is very profitable but at the same time very difficult to maintain, some coordination mechanism in the form of direct support by public agencies may become necessary. An example of public support is related to the commitment of local-government agencies for encouraging the creation of scientific poles and parks;
- *Information technology networks*: considering that activities and resources flows among different economic actors always require intensive

information exchanges, it follows that information technology, reshaping and facilitating such information flows, has recently come to occupy an important place among the coordination mechanisms employed by networks (Ebers, 1999);

- *Hierarchy and authority relations*: certain hybrids can make use of hierarchical and authoritarian coordination mechanisms in addition to other more equal relationships. For example, the coordination mechanisms that make franchising work comprise formal planning and programming activities, supervision and information systems which are similar to those employed by single firms (Mathewson and Winter,1985);
- *Planning and control systems*: some hybrids often employ control systems based on results for monitoring the observance of cooperative relations, particularly in situations of high uncertainty and unobservability of input behaviours and processes. Franchising is the inter-firm organisational form showing the highest planning and control-by-results intensity.

Hybrids as networks of relationships

It is important to mention that hybrids are also viewed as organisational *networks*. According to this idea, hybrids are seen as networks of relationships through which organisations either exchange and share resources or take advantage of economic efficiencies. It was Powell (1990) one of the most important authors who suggested the notion of network for describing new forms of organisational design and collaboration to govern economic exchanges. The author maintained that it is the simultaneous pressures towards efficiency and flexibility that pushes more and more firms to create networked organisations. These forms are different from both the transactions of markets and the hierarchical firms as networks comprise companies engaged in a complex latticework of collaborative ventures with other firms over extended periods of time. Powell uses an effective metaphor to clarify this difference: 'Surely this patterned exchange looks more like a marriage than a one-night stand, but there is no marriage license, no common household, no pooling of assets' (Powell, 1990: 301).

The distinguishing features of networks can be summarised as follows:

- Networks are more social than markets and hierarchies. They are characterised by mutual interests and reputation. They are less guided by a formal structure of authority.

- Networks imply complementarities and interdependencies to be dealt with reciprocal adaptation.
- In networks it is necessary to take a long-term perspective. This orientation enhances reciprocity.
- Networks use reciprocal patterns of communication. Useful information comes from past experience with counterparts rather than from the formal chain of command.
- Easier access to know-how, increased operational flexibility, and enhanced competitive responsiveness are critical components that motivate participants to join and stay within a network.

In the field of economic studies as a whole, the major theoretical strands of research on networks include concepts and methods borrowed from industrial economics, resource dependence theory, neo-institutional theory, industrial marketing, negotiation analysis, organisational behaviour, historical and evolutionary approaches, population ecology, and radical and Marxian studies (Grandori and Soda, 1995). All these perspectives have helped both theorists and managers to develop a more comprehensive overview on inter-organisational relationships and on their critical issues, as each of them has contributed to unveil the multiplicity of aspects connected to hybrid, networked forms of organising.

Industrial economics, being concerned with incomplete or mixed forms of 'quasi-integration', studies different classes of production costs as explanatory variables of network efficiency. According to this approach, *economies of scale* play a fundamental part in the formation of resource pooling coalitions for the supplying of common services – especially in franchising and in joint production agreements – while *economies of scope* represent the foundations for the shared use of know-how and equipment – as in the case of licensing agreements – and *economies of specialisation and experience* explain the superiority of a network of separate enterprises vs an integrated firm – as in subcontracting.

Another approach on networks is particularly important: it is the one proposed within the *resource dependence theory* which makes provision of a broad range of networking phenomena, as in the contribution by Pfeffer and Salancik (1978), offering a review of important alternative forms of inter-firms collaborations as well as empirical evidence supporting theoretical results. The resource dependence perspective distinguishes among *types of dependence* as possible predictor of networks and, in addition to the explanatory variables suggested by organisational theorists, proposes also the strategic manipulation of transactions and games aimed at changing the interdependence relation to one's own advantage.

Dependence is a central notion also within the *neo-institutional approach*: inter-organisational forms of cooperation are created and sustained in order to avoid isolation and to gain *legitimisation* by belonging to a certain network of firms. Besides, the formation and shape of networks is affected by 'institutional embeddedness' in the sense that the relative effectiveness of networking forms is contingent to the social institutions in which they are embedded. In agreement with organisational sociology, networks are said to be sensitive to pre-existing social relationships, which constrain the underlying economic relations: actors participating to a network bear internalised values and norms whose nature is an important explanatory variable of inter-firm cooperative behaviour.

Also *industrial marketing*, whose research focus is on trade between organisations, has contributed to outline the interdependencies potentially existing between separate firms. Turnbull and Valla (1986), in particular, points out that, in industrial markets, the norm is represented by the existence of long-term and stable relationships characterised by *mutual adaptation and change*. Thus, within industrial markets, stability derives from the existence of close ties and long-term networking agreements, while competition still occurs when subsisting relationships change and new relationships are formed. The interaction model as well stresses the role of interaction processes in long-term buyer–seller transaction relationships of industrial goods, analysing principally the social exchange aspects and the dynamics of networks.

Unlike industrial marketing, *negotiation analysis* studies interaction processes and exchanges of resources and behaviours, in order to understand which are the forms adopted for regulating them. With respect to the aforementioned approaches, the negotiation perspective adds the explanation of inter-firm coordination agreements from the point of view of the type of negotiation processes emerging within networks. Any network arrangement and any *coordination* problem can be expressed as a game, which can be used as a predictor of both network foundations and shape.

From an *organisational behaviour* viewpoint, the importance of long-term inter-organisational relationships resides in the ability of generating *cooperation and trust*: these two factors enable some different types of network structures which can adequately manage transactions only partially definable in advance. According to this perspective organisations choose to work together and closely for mutual benefit, as cooperation leads to a better overall performance.

Table 3.2 Hybrids as networks: perspectives, managerial issues and key variables.

Antecedents on networks	Issues and focus of analysis	Key explanatory variables
Industrial economics	Networks as organisational forms *economising on production costs*	(1) Economies of scale (2) Economies of scope (3) Economies of specialisation and experience
Resource dependence theory	Networks as means for *managing and leveraging on resource interdependencies*, which are also function of the width of inter-firm relationships	Strategic manipulation of transactions and games aimed at changing the interdependence relation to one's own advantage
Neo-institutional theory	Networks as inter-organisational forms of co-operation created and sustained in order to *avoid isolation and to gain legitimisation*	(1) Institutional embeddedness (2) Pre-existing social relationships (3) Values and norms of the participants
Industrial marketing	Networks as the result of *processes of interaction and mutual adaptation* between separate firms	Trading interdependencies
Negotiation analysis	Networks as means *for regulating exchanges* of resources and behaviours	Type of negotiation processes (expressible as games)
Organisational behaviour	Networks as organisational forms *generating co-operation through trust*	Better overall performance
Historical and evolutionary approach	Networks as means of *co-ordination and co-operation* (alternative to the 'visible hand') *within the processes of technological innovation*	(1) Technology innovation and related costs (2) Problems of learning
Population ecology	Networks as organisational forms for *increasing the survival chances* of firms	(1) Legitimisation (2) Public support (3) Legislation
Radical and Marxian studies	Networks as mechanisms for *reproducing élites*	(1) Power (2) Class dominance

Historical and evolutionary models, both based on the work by Alfred Chandler (1984), stress the role of inter-firm cooperation and coordination within the processes of *technological innovation*: the formation of networks is thus linked to the role of technology and learning.

Differing from all the approaches previously mentioned, the *population ecology* perspective studies specifically the causes of the endurance of inter-firm agreements, independently from the reasons of their emergence. Adopting a natural-selection perspective, *legitimisation* has been pointed out to be one of the most important variable driving the selection processes regarding networks, whose survival is also influenced by public support and legislation.

Also *radical and Marxian studies* give a completely original insight on networks: in fact, casting aside the questions of networks effectiveness and efficiency, they examine those inter-firm agreements which are based on *power* mechanisms.

A discussion of the different approaches to networks has highlighted that there exists a wide and varied conceptual framework that can be helpful in understanding and explaining the most important managerial issues underlying hybrid relationships. Each of the major strands of research examined has produced explanations that partially overlap and partially compete, as shown in Table 3.2.

4

The control of
collaboration across
organisational boundaries

After having outlined the organisational and managerial dimensions of collaborative forms between firms, this chapter steps into the core of this book. It presents different forms of control for collaborating firms and illustrates how managers can select them effectively. The choice of the right mix of control mechanisms contributes to the success of collaboration across firms' boundaries.

The role of control in monitoring collaborating partners

Control has been defined in different ways. One common definition is that control is a process of regulation and monitoring for the achievement of organisational goals. It refers to the process by which one subject affects another subject by means of a wide range of bureaucratic, cultural and other informal mechanisms (Etzioni, 1965; Ouchi, 1979; Baliga and Jaeger, 1984). Different authors have used a variety of words in the literature such as 'levers of control', 'control mechanisms' and 'control systems' (Bradach and Eccles, 1989; Flamholtz, Das and Tsui, 1985; Simons, 1991; Das and Teng, 1998).

Often, when firms grow in size and involve a substantial number of units and individuals, there are forces that generate competing goals, conflicts, tensions and opportunistic behaviours. As a result, the top management needs to monitor and coordinate the activities of the various organisational subjects (Child, 1972; Mintzberg, 1979; Geringer and Hebert, 1989). This suggests why contributors have concentrated their analysis on this issue for many years (Etzioni, 1961; Tannebaum, 1968; Child, 1972; Lorange and Scott Morton, 1974; Giglioni and Bedeian, 1974; Ouchi and Maguire, 1975; Edstrom and Galbraith, 1977; Ouchi, 1978; Vancil, 1979; Merchant, 1982; Schreyogg and Steinmann, 1987; Green and Welsh, 1988).

One area that has been only recently explored and has received only unsystematic attention is that of control in collaborative relationships between firms. This topic was first investigated by West (1959), who identified potential tensions and contrasts between partners. According to the author, without effective control systems, partners are likely to experience great difficulty in managing relationships with partners. Yet, despite these early considerations, the topic of control in inter-organisational relationships has been only marginally investigated, without any explicit attempt to provide an integrative approach to the issue.

Relevant to this is the question of what the role of control in the relationships between firms may be. Drawing on Fisher (1995), the principal aim of control can be seen as creating the conditions that affect the partners' behaviour in achieving predetermined results. In fact, firms establish inter-organisational relationships for realising mutually beneficial results by cooperatively performing value-creating activities. A second purpose relates to the coordination of interdependent tasks between partners. As the inter-firm tasks become more interrelated and more uncertain, the need for coor-dination and joint decisions increases (Dyer, 1996; Gulati and Singh, 1998).

These two purposes can be achieved with a variety of mechanisms, ranging from formal to informal controls and from process to outcome controls. These different forms of control are strictly interlinked and combine formal, explicitly designed controls with unwritten informal or social controls.

Researchers in the area of management control have indicated two alterna-tive modes of control: the design and use of formal rules, procedures and policies for the monitoring and rewarding of expected performance (normally referred to as formal controls); and the adoption of organisational norms, val-ues and culture (usually labelled as informal or social controls) (Eisenhardt, 1985; Das and Teng, 2001).

Formal controls include behaviour and output control mechanisms (Ouchi, 1979; Eisenhardt, 1985).

Behaviour control

Behaviour control concentrates on the process that transforms appropriate actions into expected outcomes. The focus is on the process itself rather than on the final output. The information relevant for carrying out a specific task is contained in rules that may refer to processes to be completed or stand-ards of output or quality. In order to implement these rules, it is necessary to monitor the actual performance, assign a value to it, and then compare the value associated to the performance with the rule expressed in quantita-tive terms to find out whether the actual performance is satisfactory. This requires a great amount of administrative resources (Ouchi, 1979).

Contributors indicate that behaviour control in collaborative relationships between firms can be conducted by means of a certain number of mecha-nisms (Geringer and Hebert, 1989; Makhija and Ganesh, 1997; Schaan, 1983; Das and Teng, 2001). Three mechanisms seem to be diffused and widely adopted: policies and procedures, structural safeguards, and staffing and training. Firstly, partner firms can monitor each other's behaviour by means of the implementation of *policies and procedures* (Littler and Leverick, 1995). These can be included in the contract, which indicates the acceptable boundaries of behaviour – what is desirable and what should be avoided. With rewards that reinforce pre-specified actions (Kirsch, 1996), partners will behave in line with the benefits that will derive from complying with these rules. Secondly, *structural safeguards* act against opportunism in the process of managing collaboration. Specific arrangements refer to reporting and checking devices, written notice of any departure from the agreement, accounting examination, cost control, quality control, arbitration clauses and lawsuit provisions. Making decisions on these structural specifications requires partners' investment of considerable time and resources during the negotiation stage. If the partners do not achieve an agreement on specific structures in the relationship, they may refer to their respective bargaining power. During the operation of the relationship, a great amount of resources and information processing capacity have to be employed for inter-partner control. Yet, rigid structural arrangements do effectively set the boundaries for the behaviour of inter-organisational partners (Heide, 1994; Das and Teng, 1998). These arrangements are particularly effective in those collaborative relationships in which a hub firm exercises some form of authority over the partners (Das and Teng, 2001). Finally, *staffing and training* are other important mechanisms to standardise behaviour in firms' partnerships. With adequate staffing procedures, partners can select people whose actions are in line with expected behaviour. In addition, they can shape people's behaviour by means of training procedures (Cyr and Schneider, 1996; Das and Teng, 2001).

Output control

This form of control is exercised by means of an accurate and reliable assessment of performance. Scholars indicate that output control can be conducted in inter-organisational collaborative relationships through three specific mechanisms: setting objectives, planning and budgeting, and final reporting and disclosure (Geringer and Hebert, 1989; Das and Teng, 2001).

First of all, *setting objectives* and performance measures are keys for exercising output control. In fact, without explicit expectations, output cannot be properly evaluated. The capability of defining objectives puts the partner in a position to exercise control on what is a desirable performance. In this respect, it is worth mentioning that equity stake does not automatically allow the power to set objectives. This ability is the result of shared agreement between the partners (Geringer and Hebert, 1989; Blodgett, 1991; Das and Teng, 2001). Normally, in collaborative relationships, partners aim at defining goals with a high degree of formalisation. These objectives may be either short-term or long-term oriented. Those that would like to have a high level of control over partners would select a short-term perspective because performance can be monitored more frequently against immediate objectives. However, as explicit objectives are difficult to define at the beginning of the relationship, partners will focus more on an effective goal-setting process with specific attention on congruence, specificity, communication, internalisation and completeness of goals. Eisenhardt (1985) and Ouchi (1979) stressed that defining goals is a relevant part of the control process because results have to be evaluated by comparison with the pre-existing objectives. Clear objectives not only contribute to indicating future direction in the inter-organisational relationship, but will also facilitate the definition of specific rules and regulations. However, partners may not achieve full agreement on the goals of the partnership because these goals may not effectively meet their respective interests. So, in a context characterised by information asymmetry and where opportunistic behaviour may be undertaken, partners often accept a certain degree of goal ambiguity. Often, this creates an environment that is fruitful for the activation of forms of cooperation with other firms. If this is the case, the negative effects deriving from defining specific goals, at the expense of flexibility, may be greater than the benefits of better control. Therefore, the process of goal setting may represent an effective social control mechanism in strategic inter-organisational relationships (Das and Teng, 1998).

Together with goal setting, *planning and budgeting* can also contribute to ensuring that the actions of the partners are desirable. They specify the objectives and set the direction of members' actions. Through these mechanisms, firms make sure that adequate resources and managerial support are assigned to the pursuit of inter-organisational objectives. Finally, partner firms use *financial reporting and disclosure* as a means to control outcome achievements. In this way, they ensure that outputs are as transparent as possible and if they are not met, they can be enforced through legal action (Das and Teng, 2001).

Social control

Apart from the above-mentioned forms of control, there are also other forms which have the objective of minimising discrepancies in the goal preferences of partner firms by means of 'soft' methods such as creating shared values, a common culture and a clan-like environment. These controls, normally referred to as social or clan controls, usually differ from formal controls because neither the behaviour nor the output is specified in advance.

In this form of control, no specific constraints are indicated as to which actions can be carried out or which actions are not allowed. The process of setting objectives is widely decentralised and changing in nature. Thanks to a socialisation and consensus-making process, subjects are committed to the achievement of shared goals, and common perspectives contribute to influencing strongly the actions of individuals (Ouchi, 1979; Kirsch, 1996; Das and Teng, 2001). The key aspect of social control is organisational culture, which gives a sense of control because it harmonises the way in which different subjects process information and react to the environment, thereby increasing the degree of behaviour predictability. As individuals' actions are shaped by their shared values and norms, they voluntarily act in a way that is in line with the other individuals' expectations. In cooperative relationships between firms, the management of organisational culture is at the same time a challenge and an opportunity. It is a *challenge* because it requires the combination and harmonisation of two or more different organisational cultures. Cultural inconsistency has led many inter-firm relationships to fail, because their values and beliefs were too different to be combined and transformed into one single culture. Acculturation (or cultural diffusion) allows to overcome inconsistencies through integration, assimilation, separation and deculturation. In inter-organisational relationships, the choice of which of the specific mode to use may not be shared among partners and can produce stress that may terminate with the conclusion of the relationships. This is typical in relationships in which one of the partners has a central role. In fact, as partners remain independent organisations, they are afraid of losing their own organisational identity. The challenge is therefore to make cultural blending work, while largely preserving the separate cultures. Organisational culture is also an *opportunity* because when goal incongruence and task complexity are particularly high, behavioural and output control are ineffective and a higher level of control generated by blending norms and values is needed. The key seems to be in the socialisation process between managers, which leads to more effective integration among partners, thus enabling them to familiarise themselves with each other's organisational culture (Das and Teng, 1998).

Two specific social mechanisms can be used to achieve integration: participatory decision-making (Grandori, 1997) and cultural activities (Das and Teng, 2001). *Participatory decision-making* guarantees that the expectations of each partner are clear and incorporated into joint goals and plans. In fact, in the process, partners interact to gain a better understanding of each other and gradually form a consensus, being less motivated to deviate from agreed-upon objectives. Participation ensures that potential conflicts are minimised and that more cooperative attitudes of partners are facilitated (Das and Teng, 1998). *Cultural activities* refer to the development of common norms and beliefs. These informal tools are effective ways to transform organisational ideals into behavioural models that indicate proper action (Das and Teng, 2001).

Task characteristics as determinants of control choices

One of the key variables that has been investigated by organisational theorists to explain the choice of control modes is interdependence. The core idea is that different degrees of interdependence need to be coordinated with different mechanisms (March and Simon, 1958; Thompson, 1967). Gulati and Singh (1998) emphasise the relevance of using control mechanisms for managing task interdependence in collaborative inter-firm relationships by arguing that 'concerns about anticipated coordination costs are particularly salient in alliances, which can entail significant coordination of activities between partners and yet have to be managed without the benefits of structures and systems available in traditional hierarchies' (p. 784).

There are four different types of interdependence (Thompson, 1967; Grandori, 1997):

- The first type is *pooled interdependence.* This refers to a relation in which each part renders a discrete contribution to the whole and is supported by the whole, thus indicating that there is a link between the parties because they belong to same organisation. For this reason, it is assumed that the actions of parties are aligned and that there are some boundaries to their behaviour under conditions of effectiveness. In this case, coordination is achieved through communications, rules and procedures that describe desirable actions, and through some common staff to support these activities. When applying this concept to inter-firm relationships, it relates to a context in which different firms make use of the same pooled resources (administrative structures, technology, organisational capabilities and so on). However, if the preferences and objectives of the parties do not differ substantially and control is characterised by a low number of participants and simplicity of activities, tasks can still be regulated by means of direct communication and control among members (Varian, 1990; Grandori, 1997). Alternatively, if the partners of the relationship aim at reducing their corresponding contributions to the whole and they have incentives to free-ride, then the use of a supervisory hierarchy has proven to be effective and efficient for all members (Alchian and Demsetz, 1972), provided that the activities are not complex and differentiated (Grandori, 1997).

- When activities incorporate complexity and differentiation, as in the case of combinations of different competencies to the same problem, the interlink between the parties is labelled *intensive interdependence* (Thompson, 1967; Grandori, 1997). The effective regulation of this inter-dependence requires a more complex form of coordination, because parties have to adjust reciprocally in real time and extract effective con-tributions from partners (Thompson, 1967; Avadikian, Cohendet and Llerena, 1993). To these ends, mutual adjustment and group decision-making may be adopted; however, control cannot be solved simply by means of monitoring and when the activities are difficult to observe and assess a shift to alignment of goals and preferences is to be introduced (Ouchi, 1980; Fama and Jensen, 1983; Grandori, 1997).

Apart from these forms of interdependence deriving from joint resources or actions, there are some other forms of interdependence that are more related to the regulation of transactions.

- The simplest type of transactional interdependence is represented by *sequential interdependence*. This constitutes a situation in which the output of an activity of a subject is the input for an activity of a second subject. It is the transfer of goods and services from one stage or activity A to another stage or activity B (Thompson, 1967; Williamson, 1981). These contexts are effectively coordinated by means of programming, especially when time constraints and capacity saturation problems are in place (Thompson, 1967; Grandori, 1997).
- A more complicated form of interdependence – *reciprocal interdepend-ence* – is in place when the transfers of goods and services are two-way, i.e. the output of one party becomes the input for the other and vice versa. These situations, though, are not difficult to control if the activities are known or predictable, and can be regulated by more complicated pro-grammes. However, additional coordination mechanisms are needed if activities are characterised by frequent exceptions and the lack of prede-fined cognitive schemes for solving them (Perrow, 1967). These are lateral ad hoc information exchanges and the use of specific problem solving

competences. Superordinate units dealing with exceptions are effective when they can control the relevant competencies unilaterally; alternatively, lateral relations, liaison roles and integration units are required when competencies are spread over the organisation and uncertainty originates more from cognitive complexity rather than simply from variability and exceptions (Galbraith, 1977; Grandori, 1997). Examples of inter-firm reciprocal interdependence are represented by transactions in which one party is producing something that is tailored specifically for a second party, who has provided indications to the first. The first party can act only if the second party provides inputs or transfers elements of know-how. Subcontracting relationships possess these characteristics. In the regulation of a complex network of transactions typical of the construction industry, relatively formalised and extensive systems of rules and supervisory hierarchical roles have proven to be efficient and effective. For instance, contracts between the construction firm and its customers typically specify a third party for finding technical solutions that mediate between the interests of the various parties; in addition, the relationships between the main contractor and its subcontractors are typically regulated by contracts contemplating how the main contractor will exercise supervision over the adoption of specific production plans and procedures (Williamson, 1979; Eccles, 1981; Albino et al., 1989; Grandori, 1997). Figure 4.1 summarises these arguments.

Two other variables that have been investigated by traditional contingency organisational literature for the selection of an appropriate control mode are

Pooled	Intensive
Communication and decision procedures Mutual monitoring or supervisory hierarchy	Group decision making Mutual monitoring
Sequential	**Reciprocal**
Programming Hierarchical decision making for inter-unit adjustment	Integration and liason roles Authority by exception and residual arbitration

Figure 4.1 Interdependence and control modes
(*Source*: Adapted from Grandori, 1997).

the knowledge of the transformation process (or task programmability) and the output measurability (Thompson, 1967; Ouchi, 1979; Eisenhardt, 1985):

- *Task programmability* is related to the level at which it is possible to understand the different actions of the transformation process and of their connections.
- *Output measurability* refers to the ability to measure precisely and objectively the outputs of a specific process.

In collaborative relationships between firms, the combinations of these two task characteristics seem to accord to different types of perceived risk. More specifically:

- In a context of high task programmability and low outcome measurability, the relationship seems to be characterised by *relational risk* (situation type 1). This risk refers to the probability and consequences of not having satisfactory cooperation. It arises because of the various partners having different individual interests, which are not necessarily congruent. This may lead to opportunistic behaviours like shirking, cheating, distorting information, appropriating resources and so on. Partners may have hidden agendas – e.g. secretly learning valuable knowledge and eventually taking over a target firm – which may subsequently create serious problems in cooperation and turn into low commitment (Das and Teng, 1996, 2001).
- When task programmability is low and output measurability is high, partners may perceive the presence of *performance risk* (situation type 2). This form of risk relates to the probability and consequences of alliance objectives not being achieved, despite satisfactory cooperation among partner firms (Das and Teng, 1996). For example, despite a strong commitment to learn, partners may fail to achieve effective learning and knowledge transfer. Factors that may contribute to generating this perception of risk include rivalry, new entrants, demand fluctuations, changing government policies, a lack of competence of the partner firms and so on.
- When both dimensions are at the low end, *relational* and *performance* risks are perceived at the same time (situation type 3).

When it is difficult to measure the outcomes of opportunistic behaviour and relational conflicts in a precise and objective manner but managers understand the process by which opportunistic behaviour affects the relationship in an adverse manner (situation type 1), relational risk can be effectively reduced by behaviour control. In fact, as relational risk is about partners' opportunistic behaviour and ineffective cooperation, behaviour control mechanisms or ex post deterrents, such as explicit clauses about information exchange and usage, should be adopted to regulate the actions of partners to prevent major surprises.

Alternatively, when the knowledge of the transformation process in relation to the incidence of performance risk tends to be limited – neither the most important sources of performance risk nor the unfolding of performance risk can be easily understood – and partners have developed consensus on objectives and output measures through negotiations (situation type 2), output control appears to be appropriate. This form of control helps to orient the attention of managers to key performance indicators, so that they may react as quickly as possible when performance risk rises to dangerous levels.

Finally, social control is most valuable when both output measurability and knowledge of the transformation process are low, and both relational and performance risks are in place (situation type 3). In this case, neither behaviour control not output control is appropriate, because both behaviour and output measures are unclear. Social control, in contrast, is characterised by a sufficient level of ambiguity at the beginning, allowing members to develop consensus subsequently. Organisations can, thus, overcome the issue of not being able to measure either behaviour or the outcome of such behaviour, while still being able to influence the behaviour of the partners for their own benefit. The implication is that social control can potentially deal with relational risk and performance risk simultaneously. This is so because at the beginning it may reduce the risk of non-cooperation through the establishment of shared values, thus deterring partner firms from acting opportunistically. In addition, it may reduce performance risk, because it encourages partners to lay out reasonable and achievable goals (Das and Teng, 2001). Figure 4.2 summarises these arguments.

Finally, the strategic literature has investigated two alternative variables that seem to act as antecedents of the control choices: process specificity and expertise specificity (Subramani and Henderson, 1999).

- *Process specificity* relates to the degree to which the critical processes of one firm are specific to the requirements of the other firm in a vertical inter-organisational exchange. Specialised processes are represented by routines and operating procedures that have been specifically developed

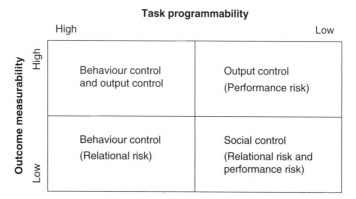

Figure 4.2 Output measurability, task programmability and control modes (*Source*: Das and Teng, 2001a).

for dealing with certain conditions occurring in specific transactions, such as new product introduction, customer service, quality control and so on. The adoption of specific information technologies often generates this type of customised process.

• *Expert specificity* refers to the degree to which a firms' critical areas of expertise are specific to the requirements of a particular firm in the collaborative inter-organisational exchanges. It is the organisation's ability to access and use extensive repositories of prior knowledge that might be related to competitive analysis, strategy formulation and new product conception (Nonaka, 1994; von Hippel, 1994). Specialised expertise is generated by means of social processes that foster the validation, refinement and enrichment of knowledge in the context of action (Nonaka, 1994; Subramani and Henderson, 1999). At an organisational level, the customisation of expertise occurs through the use of organisational resources to interpret perspectives and norms, and derives from social factors that are unique in a specific transaction context.

Process specificity and expert specificity generate four different situations:

• The situation in which both the levels of process specificity and expertise specificity are low is termed *market exchange*.
• The opposite, reflecting a high level of deployment of both specialised processes and specialised expertise in the exchange, is labelled *strategic relationship*.

- The intermediate forms are termed *expertise dominant* when the expertise specificity is high and process specificity is low, and *process dominant* when the situation is reversed.

These typologies have an impact on some characteristics of control modes that are employed for managing inter-organisational relationships: patterns of communication, long-term orientation, patterns of information technology use and relational norms.

More specifically, with reference to the *patterns of communication*, while the levels of structured and routine communication across the four types are similar, the exchange of unstructured and rich information is higher for strategic relationships and expertise-dominant ones. This suggests that a basic level of structured communication is necessary in inter-firm relationships but that this is combined with contextual information exchanges when expert specificity is high.

The *long-term orientation* of management control systems tends to prevail in expertise domination and decreases gradually in strategic relationships, market exchanges and process-dominant exchanges.

With reference to *information technologies*, there are no significant differences for basic electronic linkages (i.e. computer ordering and communication of routine messages). This suggests that information technology use is emerging as a norm in the management of all inter-firm collaborative exchanges (Lewis, 1995). In contrast, the use of information technology for process integration shows the highest levels for expertise-dominant exchanges, the lowest levels for process-dominant exchanges and intermediate levels for market exchanges and strategic relationships. Information technology use for learning and expertise leverage tends to be at the highest levels for expertise deployment, followed by strategic relationships and market exchanges. The average levels of this pattern of information technology use are lowest among the three information technology use patterns.

Finally, *relational norms* vary significantly among the different typologies. Process-dominant exchanges have the lowest levels of relational norms. Process-dominant exchanges, market exchanges and expertise-dominant exchanges are arrayed in increasing order, with strategic relationships having the highest levels of relational norms. This suggests that relational norms are gradually increasing with the introduction and use of unique and customised knowledge (Subramani and Henderson, 1999). Figure 4.3 summarises the conclusions described here.

Knowledge specificity

	Low	High
High Process specificity	**Process Dominant** Structured and routine communication H Unstructured and rich info L L/T orientation M IT for basic linkages H IT for process integration L IT for learning L Relational norms L	**Strategic Relationship** Structured and routine communication H Unstructured and rich info H L/T orientation M IT for basic linkages H IT for process integration M IT for learning M Relational norms H
Low	**Market Exchange** Structured and routine communication H Unstructured and rich info L L/T orientation M IT for basic linkages H IT for process integration M IT for learning M Relational norms M	**Expertise Dominant** Structured and routine communication H Unstructured and rich info H L/T orientation H IT for basic linkages H IT for process integration H IT for learning H Relational norms M

L = low   M = medium   H = high

Figure 4.3   Knowledge specificity, process specificity and characteristics of management control systems
(*Source*: Adapted from Subramani and Henderson, 1999).

Types of alliance as determinants of inter-partner control modes

Researchers have identified different criteria to classify inter-organisational arrangements. One classification that has gained wide consensus and that is useful to deal with control problems is one that distinguishes between joint ventures, minority equity alliances and non-equity alliances (Birnberg, 1998; Killing, 1988; Yoshino and Rangan, 1995; Das and Teng, 2001a).

Joint ventures can be defined as separately incorporated entities created and shared by the partners. The use of joint ventures is appropriate when relational risk and performance risk are both low. In fact, with reference to relational risk, joint ventures are considered a fertile context for undesired knowledge transfers. One of the reasons that firms start a joint venture is to have access to the other partner's superior knowledge and technology. Nevertheless, as firms work closely with each other, the collaboration can be a channel for secretly capturing the other partner's technology. Parties are exposed to each other in terms of tacit knowledge, technology and other valuable resources. Therefore, some firms may unintentionally lose control of their core competencies and this may lead to an unplanned termination. With reference to performance risk, joint ventures can generate strong negative economic consequences deriving from their failure. In fact, joint ventures require a lot of resources for the creation of a separate entity and for getting it started. A new organisation has to be set up, the board of directors constituted and senior level management staffed. Because of these additional costs to create new entities, joint ventures are particularly exposed to performance risk. In addition, joint ventures are based on shared equity ownership, so that possible losses from a failing joint venture tend to be high. On the one hand, the investments made cannot easily be redirected to other business opportunities. On the other hand, as partners are deeply involved in the venture, the process for separating or exiting tend to be time consuming and resource consuming. Finally, high performance risk may also derive from the high governance costs, as a result of low strategic flexibility and cultural differences. In sum, as joint ventures are potentially exposed to a high level of relational and performance risk, they are preferred when both risks are low (Das and Teng, 2001b).

Minority equity alliances relate to one or more partners taking equity positions, without creating a new legal entity. For example, one firm may sign a licensing agreement and have an equity acquisition at the same time. These forms of inter-organisational relationship are particularly effective in dealing with relational risk. Two reasons explain this conclusion. The first one is that shared ownership aligns the interest and incentives of parent firms. The second one is that as opportunistic behaviour stems mainly from performance ambiguity, and minority equity contributes to reducing this ambiguity – because they provide a mechanism for distributing residuals when ex ante contractual agreements cannot be written to specify or enforce a division of returns – the opportunistic behaviour will be discouraged (Teece, 1992). By contrast, minority equity alliances are not effective in dealing with performance risk. In fact, first, ending an alliance when there is an equity investment may be particularly complicated. Second, minority equity alliances are characterised by high governance costs. Shared ownership leads to joint decision-making and distribution of control, which, in turn, complicate the management process and reduce strategic flexibility (Harrigan, 1988; Killing, 1988; Das and Teng, 2001b).

Non-equity alliances are contractual arrangements that do not involve any equity and ownership transfer. They can be distinguished in bilateral contract-based alliances (such as, for example, joint production, joint marketing and promotion, and joint research and development) and unilateral contract-based alliances (such as, for example, licensing, subcontracting and distribution agreement). The first form of non-equity alliance is not effective in dealing with relational risk, but it is appropriate for controlling performance risk. In fact, even if it is possible to rely on contractual agreements and institutional mechanisms to foster responsible behaviour, without shared ownership it is more difficult to align partners' interests and distribute residual benefits. By contrast, they are useful for coping with performance risk because they are flexible and easy to restructure, modify and terminate. The second form is characterised by a limited engagement – so that each party is involved in implementing its part of the contractual agreement – and tends to be preferred when both relational risk and performance risk are high. In fact, the low level of engagement minimises the danger of unintended technology dissemination, shirking and cultural clash (relational risk). In addition, the ease with which it can be terminated minimises the consequence of potential failures (Das and Teng, 2001b).

In sum, the various inter-organisational relationships are suitable in contexts characterised by different levels of relational and performance risk. Therefore, as suggested in the previous section, they require different control mechanisms.

Behaviour control tends to be adopted more in equity inter-organisational relationships than in non-equity inter-organisational relationships. The reason for this is that in this latter category of relationships, collaboration is based on well-defined agreements, which can be more easily supported by output control. One example of this is represented by long-term supplier agreements in which partners do not normally try to affect each other's behaviour, as long as standard products and services meet the pre-specified requirements. By contrast, in equity alliances, the nature of cooperation is more complex and the risk of opportunistic behaviour is higher. Therefore, a closer control over the cooperative process is required. With behavioural mechanisms, this control is warranted (Garcia-Canal, 1996; Das and Teng, 2001a).

Output control tends to be adopted in all three types of inter-organisational relationship. More specifically, in joint ventures, there tends to be shared agreement on what success means and the output takes the form of financial and market-based indicators. This is not the case in minority equity alliances and non-equity alliances in which the objectives of the partners may not match. For example, if one firm invests in another, it is normally interested in return on investment or stock prices as output indicators, while the firm object of the investment may be aimed more at achieving a higher market share. The same thing happens in non-equity alliances. Take, for instance, co-marketing agreements, in which the output measure of one partner may be focused on output measures related to establishing a market channel, while those of the other partner may be related to the overall market-share development (Das and Teng, 2001a).

Finally, *social control* is particularly suitable for joint ventures. In fact, as these latter are organisationally independent entities in which partner firms collaborate tightly together, a clan-like environment can be created. Mechanisms like socialisation and interaction, thus, contribute to activating a process of creating enduring consensus (Das and Teng, 2001a).

The relationship between trust and control

The management literature has argued that trust is an important aspect of collaboration between firms (Das and Teng, 1998; Ring and Van de Ven, 1992; Sydow and Windeler, 1998). Different typologies of trust have been described by different contributions.

- *Goodwill trust* has been defined as the expectation that one entity has moral obligations and responsibility to demonstrate a special concern for their partner's interest (Barber, 1983). It is related to the reputation of a certain firm for dealing fairly and cooperating in good faith, rather than behaving opportunistically (Das and Teng, 2001).
- *Competent trust* refers to the expectation of technically competent role performance (Barber, 1983). It is the confidence that the partner is capable of accomplishing given tasks in inter-organisational relationships (Das and Teng, 2001).
- *Calculus-based trust* is strictly connected to the two previous definitions of trust but it is considered to be the result of the collection of credible information about another's goodwill and competencies. It refers also to opportunities for deterrence whenever malfeasance may occur, such as withdrawing future business opportunities and diffusing information about one's behaviour among partners, affecting other current and future relationships with the partner.
- *Relational trust* derives from continuous interaction between partners and is related to the information that the trustor is able to collect from the trustee within the relationship itself.

- Finally, *institution-based trust* concerns institutional controls to which the relationship is subject, such as the ability to rely on legal forms (when a contract is involved it is called contract-based trust) and societal norms and values (Noteboom, 1996; Roussau et al., 1998; van der Meer-Kooistra and Vosselman, 2000).

One of the most debated questions in the inter-organisational relationships literature is the association between trust and formal control mechanisms. One view is that trust is a substitute for control. More trust results in less use of formal control mechanisms and vice versa. Furthermore, the use of formal controls is argued to signal one's trust in another. Extensive use of formal control suggests a lack of belief in one's goodwill or competence and therefore results in a damaging effect on relational trust (Das and Teng, 1998; Dekker, 2004). For example, Ring and Van de Ven (1994) discuss the substitutive relationship between formal legal contracts (control) and psychological contracts[1] (trust) in collaborative relationships between firms.

Some contributors have considered trust to be a determinant for the level and form of control. Mutual trust is seen as a pre-condition for loosening control in international joint ventures (Yan and Gray, 1994) while the lack of trust between (or among) international joint venture partners is considered a prerequisite for relatively tight and broad control (Groot and Merchant, 2000).

Other authors suggest that a simple linear inverse relationship between trust and control does not exist. On the contrary, the association between trust and control is far more complex and while, to some extent, control and trust must be alternatives, the relationship between them is far from being a simple inverse one (Das and Teng, 1998; Tomkins, 2001; Coletti, Sedatole and Towry, 2005). Tomkins (2001), for example, suggests that the relationship between trust and control is different at various stages of the relationship life cycle and assumes an inverted U-shape: at the beginning of the relationship, trust and control are additively related, while later on they become substitutes.

Finally, a more extreme position is that proposed by Das and Teng (1998), who suggest a complementary relationship between trust and control: an increase in the level of either trust or formal control simply results in a higher level of control. They argue that trust and control are instrumental in

---

[1] "Psychological contracts consist of un-formalized and inexplicit sets of congruent expectations and assumptions that parties have on each other's prerogatives and obligations" (Ring and Van de Ven, 1994).

achieving a high level of confidence, so they jointly contribute to the total level of reliance one part has in partner cooperation. They also note that to have effective control over a partner in an inter-organisational relationship, a certain level of trust is needed. Trust helps in reducing the level of resistance and in building harmony in the 'controller–controlled' relationship. The use of formal control mechanisms may actually enhance a trusting relationship, by narrowing the domain of risk and by providing more objective perform-ance measures.

Collaborative information sharing across organisational boundaries

Together with the choice of control mechanisms, another critical issue affecting the management of collaborative relationships is information sharing. In this chapter, we complete the theoretical framework of our book by describing the preconditions, challenges and practices related to the effective exchange of accounting information for sustaining firms' collaboration. More specifically, we will focus our discussion on how accounting information exchanges across organisational boundaries may be used for the following purposes: collaborative planning and budgeting, inter-firm performance measurement and inter-organisational cost management. In addition, a networked-based approach to the design of inter-organisational accounting information flows between collaborating partners will be presented.

Achieving transparency in collaborative relationships through accounting information exchanges: the state-of-the-art

There is an extensive on-going discussion on the appropriateness of revealing a firm's proprietary information to other firms. The operations management literature has defined inter-organisational information sharing – including real-time information about material flows, order entry, shipping, and billing, as well as collaborative forecasts and plans (Marquez et al. 2004) – as fundamental to achieve partners' integration. In particular, supply chain management literature has stressed the advantages that can be reached by all partners through cooperation and information sharing, both in terms of costs reductions and of improved differentiation (Griffin and Hauser, 1996; Yu et al., 2001; Petersen et al., 2005).

In the management accounting literature, the idea of disclosing proprietary information to relevant partners has been labelled as open-book accounting. This expression indicates transparency on cost information, including data that would be kept secret by each partner for use in negotiations (Lamming, 1993: 214). Disclosing cost data to partners is a practice that appeared together with lean production and supply in the 1990s. So far, open-book accounting has been used by Japanese and by Western firms. The former, however, seem to require more detailed cost data disclosure than the latter (Munday, 1992; Kajüter and Kulmala, 2005: 183).

According to Kulmala (2002), there are different circumstances that would emphasise the need for open-book accounting. These are related to planning, goal setting and control at an inter-organisational level. More specifically,

open-book accounting could be used: to support pricing and offer calcula-
tions, to control the costs of resources and the profitability of products and
customers, to select product mix, for make-or-buy and outsourcing decision,
for product development decision, for the management of operations, to
increase the cost awareness among partner organisations and for collaborative budgeting and financial planning.

In addition to these situations, open-book accounting can be used to increase
the strength of a partnership. A firm reveals its proprietary information to
another firm in order to show commitment, to strengthen its position among
competing firms, to learn about the other firm's operations, and to conduct
joint cost reduction efforts. As expressed by Seal et al. (1999), open-book
accounting is decisive in the establishment of cooperative and trusting inter-
organisational agreements: 'An ideal role for management accounting would
seem to be in an open-book agreement whereby both parties can inspect each
partner's revenues and costs' (Seal et al., 1999: 321).

Interestingly, it has also been shown that the use of accounting information
between partners for discussing possible improvements along the value chain
is different from the use of accounting for coordination in a hierarchical setting, where one party can use information for developing directives for another.
The evidence reveals a different use of accounting information for coordinating inter-organisational interactions, which is based on joint communication,
cooperation and negotiation between the parties (Dekker, 2003, 2004).

By increasing information transparency between partners, open-book
accounting can also support the use of inter-organisational collaborative
budgeting and planning, cross-border performance evaluation as well as
cost accounting techniques. In the following of this chapter, we identify and
describe the most commonly used planning, performance measurement and
costing practices and techniques associated with inter-organisational information sharing in collaborative inter-firm settings.

Extending budgets and programs across organisational boundaries

When collaborating firms share proprietary information to prepare a common budget or plan, the term 'collaborative planning' is usually employed.
This term indicates a practice carried on by partners who aim at jointly
fine-tuning their programs and coordinating operations to reduce the time

between customer demand and production response. In order to do so, parties give one another visibility to sales forecasts, on the commercial side, and to manufacturing plans on the production side. Such collaborative information sharing may occur with reference to both strategic planning and strategy modelling activities and operative planning and rolling forecasting.

Strategy definition and planning are aimed at defining a collaborative strategy between the partners and the ground rules for the collaborative relationship. The main outcome of this activity are the definition of the joint strategy, of related strategic objectives and measures, usually in the form of a business plan.

With reference to the operative planning and forecasting cycle, partners collaborate and discuss in order to propose and concur on a joint operational plan. This means that, for example, the partner responsible for specific manufacturing activities shares its production forecasts and sends a planning sheet to the other partners (who, in turn, may be responsible for other production activities, or for product development, distribution, and so on) for their input. Information from customers to forecast demand and actual demand commitments are included, as well as supplier capacity plans. Ideally this should lead to the internal and external alignment of demand and supply plans. As a consequence of these consultations and negotiations, a joint operative plan is defined, based on the information that each partner shares with all the others. As a final step, collaborating firms need to evaluate the coherence of the strategic plan and the operational plan.

Different approaches have been proposed to enhance cooperation by leveraging on joint programming. One model that has received a quite high consensus among firms is the collaborative planning, forecasting and replenishment (CPFR) one,[1] providing a structure for the flow of information, goods, and services and establishing some guidelines for enterprises to integrate their planning processes across corporate boundaries. In fact, this business practice is focused on how to organise upstream value chain activities carried on by multiple partners to enhance their responsiveness in the planning and fulfilment of customer demand. It is founded on a framework for integrating a firm's planning process with that of its partner, with respect to supply, distribution and selling activities, which, in turn, is based on the idea of

---

[1]CPFR is a registered trademark of the Voluntary Interindustry Commerce Standards (VICS) Association.

real-time information visibility inside and outside each partner firm.[2] Within such framework partners develop a single forecast and update it regularly, based upon data exchanged dynamically.

The guiding principles of this collaborative planning approach are (Voluntary Interindustry Commerce Standards (VICS) Association, 2002, 2004): the focus on the final customer and the achievement of a successful value chain performance as a collaborative objective; the definition of a unique and joint forecast of demand that is used to guide planning for all the value chain partners; the commitment to shared forecast and, consequently, to risk sharing.

The CPFR approach is funded on the following main activities:

- *Strategy and planning*: in this phase, partners agree on a strategic plan, and on targets as well as on the development of joint event plans for the period. In other words, the main output of this activity should be a 'Collaboration Arrangement' defining the scope of collaboration and assigning roles, responsibilities, and business goals, and a 'Joint Business Plan' detailing the most relevant choices to achieve the goals of the collaborating firms, such as inventory policy, advertising and promotions, new product launches, specific investments and so on.
- *Demand and supply management*: during which partners need to agree on a joint sales forecasting, and on order and production forecasting as well as to verify whether production and other infrastructure capacities are in line with planned operations.
- *Execution*: relates to the implementation of operating activities going from order generation to producing, stocking, shipping, delivering products to customers, recording sales transactions, make payments to suppliers and so on.
- *Analysis of tasks*: consists in the monitoring of operations and performance evaluation to understand whether predefined goals have been met and, when needed, formulate alternative strategies, adjust strategic plans and operating forecasts and define new courses of action.

More specifically, according to the VICS Association, the CPFR model comprises nine different steps including: (1) the development of a collaboration

---

[2]It is important to underline the difference between supply chain management and the CPFR approach. The former is concerned with operational aspects of the supply chain, that is, with issues such as throughput, flow time, waiting time and flexibility, while the latter is founded on collaboration and partnerships as an approach to gain competitive advantage.

agreement, (2) the definition of a joint business plan, (3) the creation of joint sales forecasts, (4) the identification of exceptions for sales forecast, (5) the resolution and collaboration on exception items, (6) the creation of a joint order forecast, (7) the identification of exceptions for order forecast, (8) the resolution and collaboration on exception items and (9) the generation of orders.

The basic idea underlying this framework is that collaboration can be improved by making decisions on the same information deriving from consensus-based forecasting and planning processes that are formally aligned and approved at an inter-organisational level. According to several surveys (VICS Association, 2002; Fraser, 2003; Weisphal et al., 2003) the benefits of sharing management accounting information with the aim of creating a joint strategic plan and joint budgets can be the following:

- enhanced relationships,
- increased sales revenues,
- higher performance,
- improved product offering,
- reliable and accurate order forecasts,
- reduction in inventories,
- alignment in rapidly resolving value chain problems,
- improved technology return on investment.

On the other hand, the creation and implementation of shared programs require some pre-requisites to guarantee their success (Saha, 2007), such as the existence of a collective system for continuous measurement of performance, as well as the implementation of contemporary cost accounting methods, as will be described in the following sections.

Inter-organisational performance measurement of collaboration

Though there is abundant literature and evidence on performance measurement within an organisation, much less can be found on the use of performance measurement tools and practices between organisations.

The issue can be approached by highlighting two complementary subjects:

(1) the first one points to the need of extending existing performance measurement tools at an inter-organisational level;

(2)   the second one refers to the use of specific key performance indicators to measure the 'quality' of collaboration and its outcomes.

Regarding the first subject, several authors (e.g. Handfield and Nichols, 1999;
Hines et al., 2000; Zimmermann, 2003; Schmitz and Platts, working paper)
maintain the importance of shared performance measurement practices to
guarantee the success of collaborative relationships. For example, Handfield
and Nichols (1999) state that performance measurement is 'the glue' that
holds a value-creating system, composed by different partners, together, as
it supports the development and formulation of joint strategies as well as the
collaborative implementation of these strategies. These same authors recom-
mend the balanced scorecard (BSC) as a performance measurement tool to
be used to integrate the measurement logics and performance judgments of
partners collaborating across the value chain.

Following this line of reasoning, Brewer and Speh (2000) propose a modi-
fied version of the BSC with the expansion of the internal perspective to
include both the 'interfunctional' and 'partnership' perspectives. In such
a way, they advocate the incorporation of integrated measures to motivate
employees to see their firm's success as dependent upon the success of their
firm's partners. These integrated measures should be conceived in a way to
span functional and firm organisational boundaries, on the one side, to give
evidence to all partners of the performance generated through the collaboration and, on the other side, to provide incentives to cooperate with partners.
Such measures would complement the non-integrated measures traditionally
included in the BSC, that is, those providing signals on critical performance
areas concerning individual firms involved in the collaboration.

Brewer and Speh (2000) also propose some value chain measures to be used
in each of the four perspectives of the BSC. Some examples are:

(1)   The customer perspective:
      – *Number of customer contact points*: As a measure of service
        quality indicating how many people the customer has to inter-
        act with to be served. The lower the number the better, as when
        many possible contact points exist in the value chain, miscom-
        munication, waste, and deferred response might occur and have
        a negative impact on customer satisfaction.
      – *Relative customer order response time*: Defined as the time nec-
        essary to respond to a customer order compared to the time
        needed by a competing supply chain. This benchmark aims at

granting that partners are always aware of what their customers expect from their collaboration on value chain activities.

- *The customer perception of flexible response*: Measures the perception of customers of the relationship between customisation and response time. This indicator is defined to capture whether the customer thinks the customised requests are executed in a timely manner through efficient coordination among the value chain partners.
- *The customer value ratio*: Indicates the customer's view of the value chain performance. This is measured as a ratio of the quality, time and flexibility perceived by the customer and the cost incurred. The formula is: (survey measures of quality, flexibility and time)/cost per order. The logic of collaborating along the value chain would aim at improving this percentage by increasing the numerator, that is, customer satisfaction, and by diminishing the denominator, that is, the unit cost of orders.

(2) The internal perspective:

- *The value chain cost of ownership*: Measures all the costs across the supply chain related to purchasing, storing inventory, low quality and delivery breakdowns.
- *The value chain cycle efficiency*: Defined as total value-added time divided by total time in the value chain. The ideal target for this measure would be 1.00. This ratio can be calculated both at the level of the whole value chain, and also within each partner firm, to detect where in the value chain problems may lie.
- *The percentage of jointly defined target costs achieved*: This is a financial measure emphasising the spending reductions that can be reached through collaboration. The calculation of this measure requires a high degree of confidence and openness with the partners.

(3) The innovation and learning perspective:

- *The product finalisation point measure*: Indicates whether the collaborating firms are able to push final product completion as close to the final customer as possible and it is calculated as the time between finalisation and customer delivery. The closer to the customer the product is finally assembled, the better the measure.
- *The product category commitment ratio*: Is a measure of 'true' collaboration and is calculated by considering at the numerator the

percentage of the seller's total product category sales that are sold to a particular customer and at the denominator the percentage of that customer's product category needs that they bought from that seller. From a collaborating partnership perspective ideally the ratio should be 1.0 as it would be a sign of an ideal balance of influence and commitment between the partners. On the contrary, in all those situations where the ratio is near to 100 (100/1) or .01 (1/100), there might be one partner able to leverage on unbalances of power to gain supplementary economic profits from the collaboration at the expense of another parties.

– *The number of shared data sets relative to total data sets*: Is a ratio indicating whether partners have invested in creating a common language and information repository to be used collaboratively by all firms in the value chain. This measure is critical because the sharing of essential business information, both accounting and non-accounting-based, is an important signal of the extent to which firms are actually collaborating.

(4) The financial perspective:

– *Profit margin by partner*: Measuring the amount of profits, as a percentage of the total profits, of each partner. Whenever there is a high difference between the profit percentages of partners, this should be investigated to understand whether it is due to a power imbalance that could be risky for collaboration.

– *The return on value chain assets*: Computed as the ratio between the sum of partners' profits and the average assets used in a certain period to support collaboration. This is a measure of the efficiency with which partners are able to coordinate the deployment of their assets (see Figure 5.1).

Regarding the second issue, that is, the use of metrics for measuring collaboration, it should be recalled that the literature on performance measurement within a single organisation already deals with questions such as opportunistic behaviour, principal-agency problems, value appropriations concerns and so on. In an inter-organisational context, these problems are more severe as there are, by definition, multiple principles per agent and several interest groups with possible departing objectives (Schmitz and Platts, working paper). It becomes thus particularly critical to measure collaboration.

On this point, based upon the results of a survey and a literature review, Zhao (2002) proposes an index of key performance indicators in an attempt

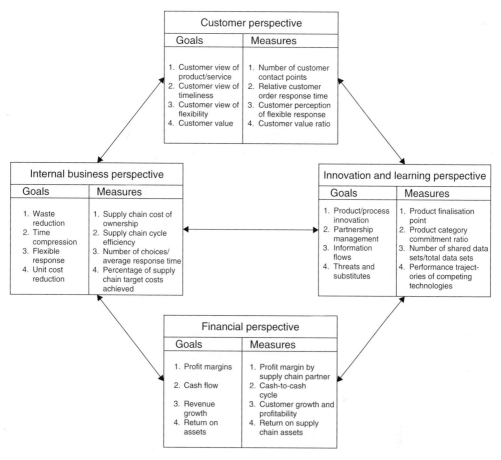

Figure 5.1 The value chain BSC
(*Source*: Brewer and Speh, 2000: 86).

to measure the performance of partnerships in terms of inter-organisational collaboration. This index is based on the certainty that mutuality is a key to success to any collaborative partnership, and, therefore, aims at capturing some important aspects of reciprocity, such as mutual understanding through communications, mutual trust, mutual benefits, mutual evaluation and sharing (Zhao, 2002: 5).

There can be metrics to measure the extent of collaboration such as:

- number of personnel contributing from each participant;
- proportion of projects/programs involving more than one participant;
- number of joint projects/programmes sharing major facilities.

Some other metrics that can be used to measure inter-organisational collaboration are referred to its underlying critical success factors (commitment, communication, sharing, trust, profitability, productivity and market share) are the following:

- *Commitment*: time and nature of contribution by partners.
- *Communication*: frequency, mode and nature of communications between partners.
- *Sharing*: frequency/amount and type of information/data exchanges between the partners.
- *Trust*: frequency of meeting one's expectation about another party's behaviour and/or having confidence in another party.
- *Profitability*: profit margins realised from collaborative projects.
- *Productivity*: number/percentage of collaborative projects finished within time and budget.
- *Market share*: percentage of market share obtained through partnerships.

As a final remark, Zhao (2002) observes that, given the peculiarities of inter-organisational collaboration, effective performance metrics are those able to push the desired values and behaviours of partners towards the achievement of their common business goals.

Cost measurement and management practices to support collaboration

Among the different uses of management accounting information in inter-organisational partnerships, the one related to inter-organisational cost measurement and management is probably the most wide-spread among firms and, as a consequence, also the most investigated in the literature.

In the following sections, we explore several techniques and practices that may support collaboration in different ways:

- The *total cost of ownership* (see below) used, at the exploratory stage of the relationship, to select partners, and, once the collaborative agreement has been established, for assessing joint projects aimed at the improvement of mutual profitability and for performance reviews and rewards of the cooperating partners.
- The *value chain analysis* (see below) employed to support cost reduction and differentiation improvement initiatives, especially in those

collaborating agreements characterised by high sequential or reciprocal interdependencies of value chain partners.

- *Inter-organisational cost management techniques* (see below) based on the *target costing* logic, applied for inter-organisational cost planning and control, mainly in those situations where collaboration is aimed at joint product design.

The total cost of ownership approach to select and monitor collaborative suppliers

In recent contributions, it has been stated that purchasing impacts significantly on the competitive position of many firms as it accounts for 60–70% of total expenditures in manufacturing and influences all the activities in a firm value chain (Herberling, 1993; Degraeve et al., 2004). Partnerships with suppliers have thus been said to represent an important solution to improve performance, although such issue has not received so far the attention it deserves from Western firms. The most advanced examples in this field are referred to Japanese firms, which have been able to obtain large cost reductions and to improve their competitive positions thanks to closer relationships with their most important suppliers. Some examples of the advantages derived from closer relationships with suppliers include (Ittner et al., 1999: 255):

(1) the reduction of product development costs through earlier availability of prototypes, higher standardisation of parts, improved fit between the product design and the supplier's manufacturing capabilities;

(2) improved quality – and consequent decrease of costs due to low quality and defects – through closer and earlier controls of parts provided by suppliers;

(3) enhanced efficiency through the incorporation of supplier-originated innovations in products and shared processes (Frazier et al., 1988: 55; Carr and Ittner, 1992: 48–50).

Starting from the experience of Japanese firms, management accounting and supplier management studies have described several mechanisms that can be used to involve suppliers into performance improvement initiatives. The use of these mechanisms is related to the need of both managing the underlying contractual uncertainty and of obtaining a higher flexibility and adaptability from closer relationships with these external partners.

There are three categories of supplier selection and monitoring practices that have been described in partnerships (Ittner et al., 1999: 254; Atkinson and Waterhouse, 1996; Gietzmann, 1996: 614–616):

(1) *frequent face-to-face contacts and meetings* between the buyer and its suppliers: regular interactions with suppliers helps decreasing the inevitable information asymmetry between the parties and enhancing the buyer's possibility to discover potential opportunistic behaviours from the supplier (Noordewier et al., 1990: 84; Gietzmann, 1996: 616);

(2) *supplier certification*, based on extensive investigation of suppliers' manufacturing operations, facilities and personnel. When a supplier is 'certified' it means that he or she is legitimated to provide goods without testing each receipt (Baiman et al., 1998);

(3) *non-price-selection criteria* founded on a total cost of ownership, including not only quoted price but also all the costs of quality and delivery deficiencies, as well as administrative requirements, net of the additional benefits of suppliers collaboration in product development and cost reduction initiatives (Carr and Ittner, 1992: 48–49; Ellram and Siferd, 1998: 57–59).

Regarding the effectiveness of such practices it has been proved that greater information sharing and intense interaction with suppliers improve purchasing performance in high uncertainty transactions (such as in partnerships), but have no impact in low uncertainty, arms-length relationships (Noordewier et al., 1990: 85). Also certification is effective only when the firm entertains a close relationship with suppliers, but not in case of arms-length relations (Baiman et al., 1998). Similarly, the advantages of using supplier selection and monitoring practices are superior to their costs only when the buyer develops strong partnerships with its suppliers.

More generally speaking, in buyer–supplier relationships, certification mechanisms and non-price selection criteria can be used to find out which are the suppliers who possess the highest commitment to the relationship and the best capabilities. In this sense, they can be considered as ex ante control mechanisms that diminish the need to use ex post controls (Ittner et al., 1999: 257; Baiman et al., 1998; Stump and Heide, 1996: 433).

One practice that is spreading among firms entertaining partnerships with their suppliers is the use of total cost of ownership, both as a selection and as a performance measurement and reward mechanism. The total cost of ownership is a cost accounting approach that examines the cost associated with purchased goods and services along the entire supply chain, from the development of a new component (when done collaboratively with a supplier) till the possible warranty claims associated with that part when the product is used by the final customer. Therefore, total cost of ownership analyses consider a broader spectrum of acquisition costs and look at life cycle costs associated with employing an item from a certain supplier, including the costs incurred once the item is in use by the buyer and by the final customer (Ellram, 1993: 3–4).

It aims at combining price and value in making sourcing decisions by quantifying all the costs involved in acquiring and using different offerings from suppliers (such as transaction costs related to purchasing activities – for example, ordering, freight, quality control – and the costs related to poor quality – for example, rejection, rework, and warranties) (Carr and Ittner, 1992; Ellram, 1995; Wouters et al., 2005: 167).

A comprehensive view on total cost of ownership items is gained by relating the cost elements to the transaction. In this way, it is possible to distinguish pre-transaction, transaction and post-transaction costs (Ellram, 1993: 7).

Pre-transaction costs include all the costs incurred prior to placing the order, such as:

- investigating alternative sources,
- adding suppliers to internal systems,
- qualifying and educating suppliers to the firm's operations (e.g. delivery methods),
- educating the firm to suppliers' operations.

Transaction costs comprise all the costs related to order placement and receipt and thus include:

- price,
- order placement,
- delivery/transportation,
- tariffs/duties,
- billing/payment,
- inspection,
- returns,
- follow up and corrections.

Post-transaction costs (in practice, the least 'recognised' costs among all the total cost of ownership items) include all the costs that occur while the supplied item is owned and used by the firm as well as by the firm's final customer. These include:

- line fallout,
- defective goods rejected before sale,
- product repair in the field,
- routine and special maintenance costs,
- repair of parts,
- loss of customer goodwill/reputation of firm.

There are four primary uses of the total cost of ownership for:

(1) supplier selection,
(2) supplier evaluation and performance measurement,
(3) supplier motivation and reward,
(4) change processes/re-engineering of interdependent activities along the supply chain.

Recently, an extension of the total cost of ownership approach has been proposed, that is the total value of ownership. This is because the definition of total cost of ownership does not consider the possible added value – deriving from a certain supplier offering – which will be produced downstream by the purchasing firm. A specific component acquired from a partner supplier may contribute to increasing the quality or the functionalities of the product in the eye of the final customer. This, in turn, may translate into a higher performance in the firm's final market as well as in an increase of its revenue potential. On this point, as exemplified by Wouters et al. (2005: 186), Dupont's SilverStone non-stick finish has a higher price than generic non-stick finishes, yet the greater durability it provides enables the cookware manufacturer to charge a higher price (to retailers and consumers) than for cookware coated with a generic non-stick finish. This is a difference that the cookware manufacturer should need to take into account when selecting and evaluating alternative suppliers. The total value of ownership would therefore consider the total cost of ownership for each specific supplier net of the performance advantages gained by the buyer in terms of value created for its customers and related additional revenues and profits.

As a final remark, it is important to underline that, nowadays, the majority of purchasing managers still seem to rely more on price information than on total cost of ownership in selecting their partner suppliers. One of the most important obstacles to the implementation of the total cost of ownership approach has been proved to be the lack willingness of cost data sharing (Ellram and Siferd, 1998; Wouters et al., 2005).

Value chain analysis to pursue competitive advantage with collaborative partners

The value chain framework is an approach for breaking down the chain of business functions into the strategically relevant activities through which value is added to products and services. In other words, this framework identifies a linked set of value-creating activities from basic raw material sources to the final consumer.

Michael Porter (1985) defined two groups of business activities:

(1) *Primary activities*: those activities that are directly concerned with manufacturing and delivering a product or a service.
(2) *Support activities*: those activities that, although not directly involved in manufacturing and delivering a product or a service, may contribute to increasing the effectiveness or efficiency of a certain business.

Primary value chain activities include:

(1) *Inbound logistics*: concerned with receiving and storing externally sourced materials, or work-in-progresses, or finished goods.
(2) *Operations*: related to the transformation of resource inputs into outputs, that is, the manufacture of products and the provision of services.
(3) *Outbound logistics*: concerned with the supply of goods and services to buyers.
(4) *Marketing and sales*: related to all the activities for informing buyers and consumers about products and services.
(5) *Service*: concerned with maintaining product/service performance after the product has been sold or the service provided to customers.

Support activities include:

(1) *Procurement*: associated with all the activities for the acquisition of those resources that are necessary for a certain business.
(2) *Technology development*: related to managing information processing and the development and protection of knowledge.
(3) *Human resource management*: concerned with selecting, training, motivating and compensating the workforce.

(4)   *Infrastructure*: including a variety of support systems and functions like finance, accounting and control, quality control, general management, etc.

Which specific activities a business undertakes is directly linked to achieving competitive advantage. Porter argued that a business can develop a sustainable competitive advantage based on cost, differentiation, or both.

A *low-cost/price strategy* focuses on providing goods or services at a lower cost than the competition, or superior goods or services at an equal cost. A strategy based on cost leadership will require a reduction in the costs associated with the value chain activities, or a reduction in the total amount of resources used. This strategy requires a tight cost-control system, and the possibility to take advantage from economies of scale and experience curve effects.

Differentiation, the second strategy for gaining competitive advantage, aims at creating a unique position for the firm in the market through provision of goods or services that are valued for their uniqueness or fit to the particular needs of a specific group of buyers. A differentiating strategy also requires on-going cost-control efforts within a strategic management emphasis geared towards differentiating offerings. For example, a business which wishes to outperform its competitors through differentiating itself through higher quality will have to perform its value chain activities better than the opposition.

Starting from this framework, Porter (1985) identified strategic cost analysis as a means to better manage the linkages within the value chain and, related to that, proposed value chain analysis. In the strategic management accounting field, Shank (1989) and Shank and Govindarajan (1992, 1993) further developed this idea, defining strategic cost management as 'the managerial use of cost information explicitly directed at one or more of the four stages of the strategic management cycle' (Shank, 1989: 48)[3] and value chain analysis as one of the three main topics of strategic cost management. More specifically, value chain analysis is a structured method for breaking up 'the chain of activities that runs from basic raw materials to end-use customers into strategically relevant segments in order to understand the behaviour of costs

---

[3] These latter are: formulating strategies; communicating strategies throughout the firm; developing and executing tactics to implement the strategies; and, finally, developing and applying controls to monitor the strategy implementation.

and the sources of differentiation' (Shank and Govindarajan, 1992: 80). Such analysis can help firms examining the value chain for strategic improvement, that is, for determining which type of competitive advantage to pursue, and how to pursue it.

Value chain analysis generally includes three phases (Shank and Govindarajan, 1993: 58):

(1) *Identify strategically relevant activities*, assign to this value activities costs, revenues and assets. Activities should defined as separate if:
    (a) they correspond to a significant amount of operating costs;
    (b) they are performed by competitors in different ways;
    (c) they have a high differentiation potential;
    (d) the cost behaviour of the activities or their cost drivers are different.

(2) *Diagnose the cost drivers* that cause the economic behaviour of each activity. In this respect, accounting information is an important constituent of value chain analysis. Several authors (Dekker, 2003, 2004; Guilding et al., 2000; Mecimore and Bell, 1995; Shank and Govindarajan, 1992, 1993) mention the use of an Activity-Based Cost (ABC) analysis as a basis for the identification of cost drivers. These latter can belong to two different categories (Riley, 1987; Shank and Govindarajan, 1993):
    (a) *Structural*, i.e. cost drivers related to strategic choices that impact on costs. There are five strategic choices that drive costs:
        (i) *Scale*: Investment size in manufacturing, research and development, and marketing;
        (ii) *Scope*: Degree of vertical integration;
        (iii) *Experience*: Previous repetitions of current work;
        (iv) *Technology*: Process technologies used at each step in value chain;
        (v) *Complexity*: Broadness of product line.
    (b) *Executional*, i.e. cost drivers related to an organisation's ability to execute successfully. The fundamental ones are:
        (i) *Work force involvement*: participation, empowerment, commitment to continuous improvement;
        (ii) *Capacity utilisation*: scale choices on plant construction;
        (iii) *Plant layout efficiency, compared to current norms;*
        (iv) *Product configuration*: design or formulation effectiveness;
        (v) *Exploiting linkages with suppliers/customers*: in relation to the value chain.

(3) *Develop a sustainable competitive advantage* by using the outcomes of the analysis either to control cost drivers better than competitors or to reconfigure the value chain. In principle, competitive advantage can be achieved either by reducing costs, while keeping value constant, or by increasing value, while keeping costs constant.

These phases can be applied either/both to the company's internal value chain or/and, with a broader view, to the industry value chain.[4]

The first one includes all the physical and technological activities within the company that add value to the product. The key for analysing it is to find out which are the activities that provide a firm with a competitive advantage, and then leverage on those advantages better than competitors. This evaluation is usually done as follows:

(1) Identify value chain activities by:
    (a) looking for discrete activities, which create value in different ways. These activities have different costs, different cost drivers, separable assets, and different personnel involved.
    (b) separating structural, procedural, and operational activities. Structural activities are those that determine the economic nature of a firm, while procedural activities concern the firm's ability to carry out the processes efficiently and effectively.
    (c) focusing on structural and procedural activities, instead of on operational activities only.
(2) Determine which activities are strategic, by identifying which product or service characteristics are better appreciated by customers.
(3) Trace costs to activities, by usually using an activity-based costing logic.
(4) Improve management of value chain activities by focusing on decreasing total costs while improving competitive advantage. This does not imply that all costs must be decreased but that all costs that do not adversely affect the competitive advantage should be reduced.

---

[4] Traditionally, the only use of ABC at an extra-organisational level was in finding how partners along the supply chain may impact on the costs and the profits of a specific firm. Organizations have ignored so far a real inter-organizational orientation that presumes a firm looks outside its boundaries to understand where, in the supply chain, activities can be improved, in terms of cost, time, or quality (LaLonde and Pohlen, 1996).

The second one, the industry value chain, is composed of all the value-creating activities within a certain industry, beginning with raw materials, and ending with a sale to a customer. In this chain, there are both many upstream and downstream linkages, each one indicating an independent, economically viable segment of the industry. In analysing the industry value chain, there are basically three/four steps:

(1) *Definition of segments within the industry value chain*: to define whether a certain linkage represents a separate segment, one needs to give a positive answer to either one of the following two questions: Is there a market for the output of this linkage, or can a price be determined easily? Are there any competitors whose activity is focused on this linkage of the value chain?

(2) *Examination of the relative position of the specific firm*: the relative strength of the position of the firm should be examined with reference to each specific separate linkage in the industry value chain. This can be done by taking into consideration various benchmarks, including industry margins, return on assets, and so on.

(3) *Analysis of the internal value chain of the firm* to find out how to improve its relative position with reference to competitors and enhance its competitive advantage by exploiting linkages between activities within the firm.

And/or

(4) *Analysis of the linkages upstream and downstream the firm's activities.* In an industry value chain, various types of external 'linkages' can be distinguished (i.e. linkages with suppliers, linkages with buyers, and so on), each one representing a potential area for improvement, either in terms of costs or in terms of profits deriving from enhanced differentiation. In fact, the existence of a linkage indicates the existence of a relationship between the performance of one activity and the performance of another activity. In other words, a linkage signals a certain degree of interdependence between upstream and downstream firms (Shank and Govindarajan, 1992). In this respect, value chain analysis is a method that can be used to manage inter-firm linkages, as it facilitates the optimisation and coordination of interdependent activities that may cross different organisational boundaries.

Therefore value chain analysis is a concept that potentially crosses organisational boundaries and includes multiple firms across the value chain, so that insights are gained into how different firms' activities are interrelated in terms of cost and differentiation.

It should be underlined that Shank and Govindarajan implicitly assume that value chain analysis is performed by one firm 'taking an external perspective', that is to say looking beyond its boundaries to its buyers and suppliers in the value chain. On the contrary, more recent contributions (Dekker, 2003, 2004) stress that outcomes are greater if partners cooperate on value chain analysis rather than performing it individually. Therefore, in inter-firm relationships, to grasp the full potential of value chain analysis, this should be carried on jointly by partners whose activities are interdependent in the value chain. In this sense, this analysis is named collaborative value chain analysis.

Dekker and Van Goor (2000) emphasise the usefulness of collaborative value chain analysis by presenting a case study in the pharmaceutical industry. They show how activity-based costing supported decisions about relocating and modifying logistics in order to increase the profits of partners along the whole supply chain. Based on this experience, they conclude that organisations' performances can benefit from the strategic exploitation of linkages with the value chains of partners and that this can be done by engaging in collaborative cost analysis.

Before concluding, it should be noted that there are two main challenges linked to putting collaborative value chain analysis in practice.

A first challenge is a very practical one, and is related to the potentially *different advancement stages of the cost accounting systems* of value chain partners. In fact, quite seldom, firms adopt accounting systems that are already designed to allocate costs to activities, according an activity-based costing logic. It is quite common to find the coexistence of accounting systems with different degrees of sophistication among the various parties along the value chain.

A second challenge can be related to *potential opportunistic behaviours or conflicts* that may arise when partners decide to share sensitive information, like cost and performance information. To face this challenge, partners need to be trustful that this information will not be used in an adversarial way. At early stages of the relationship, when likely trust is not high, oftentimes partners decide to use formal contractual agreements on profit and cost sharing, or confidentiality agreements for information exchange before deciding to carry out a collaborative value chain analysis (Dekker, 2003). On this point, the example mentioned in the previous section is quite illuminating. To increase the willingness of suppliers to participate in the collaborative value chain analysis project, Sainsbury declared that the disclosed information would not be used for direct comparisons between competitor suppliers. Of course, if Sainsbury had not respected this agreement, in turn, this would have damaged its reputation with its suppliers and would have compromised the possibility of implementing the cost improvement initiative underlined the collaborative value chain analysis.

Inter-organisational cost management techniques for collaborative networks

The objective of any cost management programme is to infuse in the firm a systematic and shared approach to cost reduction, that must begin when products or services are first conceived, continue during production activities, and end only when they are sold. When these activities are shared with external partners, the cost management programme must not limit its scope to just the boundaries of the firm but must be shared across the entire value chain.

Inter-organisational cost management may be used to achieve the collaborative management of costs throughout the value chain with the aim of improving the overall performance of each partner firm along the value chain. More specifically, inter-organisational cost management refers to a set of activities, processes, or techniques that managers can use to manage costs that cross firm boundaries. The outcomes associated with inter-organisational cost management systems include identifying ways of reducing costs and increasing revenues through activities such as joint product development and joint inter-organisational cost investigations (Cooper and Slagmulder 2004). Inter-organisational cost management techniques have a *cooperative* nature because the underlying activities are undertaken with the common goal to create value for all the involved partners through revision of cost structures at an inter-organisational level (Mouritsen et al., 2001; Coad and Cullen, 2006). More specifically, inter-organisational cost management practices may enable the coordination of inter-organisational cost reduction initiatives in three specific ways:

(1) by helping partners to find additional ways to reduce the costs of products through cooperation during *product design* (see on the left of the horizontal dimension in Figure 5.2);

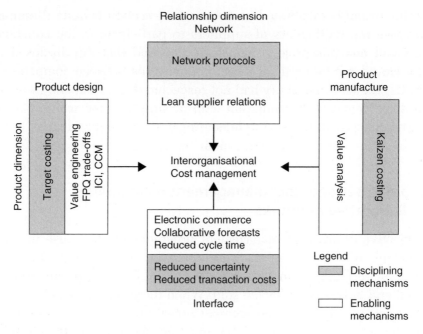

Figure 5.2   The inter-organisational cost management process
(*Source*: Cooper and Slagmulder, 1999: 10).

(2)   by helping partners to find additional ways to reduce the costs of products through cooperation during *manufacturing* (see on the right of the horizontal dimension in Figure 5.2);

(3)   by helping identifying ways to make the *interface* between partners more efficient (see the vertical dimension at the bottom of Figure 5.2).

As shown in Figure 5.2, the success of inter-organisational cost management requires the existence of both *disciplining mechanisms*, that is, those used to set cost-decreases objectives and to diffuse pressures on cost improvement initiatives for the whole supply network, and *enabling mechanisms*, that is, the ones used to support cooperation and the achievement of collective goals at the network level.

How to decrease costs during product design

Target costing represents the foundation of inter-organisational cost management when applied during the product design phase. Such cost management technique can be used with two different aims. The first one is to identify the cost at which a given product must be manufactured (the product-level target cost) given a certain target profit margin. The second one is to define the target cost down at the component level (the component-level target cost). In this second case, the buyer uses such technique to define the costs at which outsourced items, included in the final product, should be manufactured by the suppliers. Since such component-level target cost represents the 'ideal' supplier's selling price, it also becomes the signal transmitted from the buyer to its suppliers about how much and where cost reductions are needed at the component level (Cooper and Slagmulder, 1999: 182). To guarantee that the target cost is achievable by the supplier, the buyer needs to receive information from the supplier and incorporate it into the process for establishing the component-level target cost. Typical information that is required by the buyer from the supplier includes cost data and historical trends in cost reductions.

When, at the level of the whole supply network, also the suppliers use target costing, a *chained target costing system* emerges. In this chain, the outcome of a buyer's target costing system becomes the input to a supplier's target costing system. More specifically, each tier's allowable costs become the basis for setting the product-level costs and thereby setting the component-level costs for the supplier (Cooper and Slagmulder, 2003: 12). It is the firm at the top of the chain that transmits the competitive pressure it faces from the market down on its suppliers. Such pressure is based on the customers demand for quality and functionality specifications, which creates an incentive at the level of the whole supply network to focus on efficiency improvements. For a certain product, there are as many target costing chains as there are outsourced components. Typically, each chain ranges from two to six members and can take the form of either a kingdom, where there is only one end buyer, a barony, containing several end buyers, or a republic.

When cost reduction initiatives are launched in isolation, without requiring the collaboration between the buyer and the supplier, target costing systems, whether stand-alone or chained, just represent an extension of intra-firm cost management logics to an inter-firm setting (Cooper and Slagmulder, 2004). However, isolation confines the effectiveness of cost improvement initiatives to local savings.

On the contrary, chained target costing is successful when the buyer and seller's design teams can interact to modify component specifications in the product development stage to reduce costs. The nature of the interaction between the design teams depends on the type of interface existing

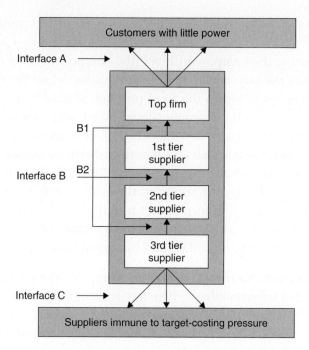

Figure 5.3 A target costing chain and the three different types of interfaces (*Source*: Cooper and Slagmulder, 1999: 210).

between the buyer and seller which, in turn, is based on the placement of each counterpart in the target costing chain. The single buyers at the top of the chain (interface A) have very little power on the supplier but as a group they can affect the success of a certain product on the market. In the middle, buyers can have a strong influence on their suppliers costs (interface B). Finally, the firm at the end of the chain is under high pressure to reduce costs and cannot transmit it to its suppliers (interface C). So, in sum, for firms placed at the beginning or in the middle of the chain, there is great room for cost reduction initiatives to be carried out with their suppliers, while at the end of the chain the firm has no power to influence the costs of its suppliers (see Figure 5.3).

To support cooperation aiming at cost reductions, inter-organisational cost management suggests some formal mechanisms for the design teams of the firms in the supply network to collaboratively interact. At the heart of such mechanisms lies *value engineering*, an organised effort for exploring how to provide the product functionalities required by the market at the same time meeting the target cost.

How to improve the coordination of manufacturing activities

To extend the disciplining logic of target costing from the product development stage to the manufacturing one, lean supply networks may employ *kaizen costing*. This technique is used to coordinate production activities by defining ex-ante cost reduction targets instead of reacting once cost decreases are needed.

There are three types of kaizen costing initiatives:

(1) *Period-specific kaizen costing*: whose objective is represented by specific reductions in the manufacturing costs in a given period. The level of cost decreases is usually set to maintain a target profitability at the firm level.

(2) *Item-specific kaizen costing*: whose objective is to reduce the costs of a given product, either new or mature, so that it can reach its target profitability in the long run.

(3) *Overhead-specific kaizen costing*: whose objective is to decrease product mix complexity, with a multi-product and multi-year focus, and by that reduce overheads.

To be performed collaboratively at an inter-organisational level, kaizen costing presupposes a tight relationship between the buyer and its suppliers, an understanding of the mutual benefits and a certain balance of power between the counterparts. Kaizen costing initiatives can be initiated either by the buyer or by the supplier.

Buyer-lead initiatives aim at reducing costs either by educating suppliers to become more efficient or by giving them access to cost savings they cannot achieve in isolation. The first method oftentimes translates into the redesign of the product or parts of it to make it more compatible with the supplier's manufacturing system. The second one consists in the identification of cheaper sources for the supplier or in leveraging on the buying power obtained by pooling together the volumes needed by the firm and its suppliers to get lower acquiring prices. In case of buyer-lead initiatives the benefits from the cost reductions are passed on to the buyer.

Supplier-lead initiatives are usually focused on component-redesign aimed at lowering costs keeping quality constant. The buyer can collaboratively support these initiatives in three ways: by changing its product to adapt to the new low-cost component, by modifying its manufacturing process to take into consideration the proposed changes in design of the component, by assisting the supplier with engineering support to help identifying potential improvements in the design of the component or in the manufacturing activities.

How to better interfaces between partners

A third approach of inter-organisational cost management is based on finding ways for managing the interfaces between the buyers and the suppliers in a more efficient manner. This is mainly done by trying to decrease uncertainty and transaction processing costs related to activities, such as order placement, inventory management, logistics and so on, crossing the boundaries of two or more firms.

There are typically four ways to *reduce transaction processing costs*:

(1) the elimination of duplicate activities;
(2) the simplification of common processes;
(3) the standardisation of high volume, routine activities common to all buyer–supplier interfaces;
(4) the automation of repetitive, high volume activities through the use of electronic commerce.

In particular, e-commerce initiatives – that is, e-purchasing of standard items, e-mailing bidding, and automated physical transfers by barcode – may help firms reducing transaction processing costs by decreasing paper documentation, eliminating data re-entry due to clerical errors, and by reducing cycle time.

Regarding uncertainty, all those initiatives aimed at reducing it have an impact on the level of inventory both for the buyer and for the supplier. In fact, as inventory represents a buffer against the suppliers' failures to deliver the goods on time and the buyers' unexpected demands, if buyer and suppliers collaborate to eliminate these causes of uncertainty they can also eliminate excess inventory. Collaboration can be achieved primarily by increasing the sharing of information and by committing to decreasing transaction processing time.

Initiatives aimed at increasing the efficiency of buyer–suppliers interfaces may be either buyer-lead or supplier-lead. The following table provides some examples derived from empirical observation (Cooper and Slagmulder, 2003).

Table 5.1 How to increase the efficiency of buyer–supplier interfaces: some examples.

Buyer-lead initiatives		Supplier-lead initiatives	
Uncertainty	Transaction processing	Uncertainty	Transaction processing
• Share forecasts • Decrease the number of special orders • Guarantee an adequate order lead time	• Define long-term purchasing contracts • Increase information sharing on joint processes	• Share forecasts • Allow the buyer to monitor order status • Reduce delivery times • Reduce production times	• Increase information sharing on joint processes

Source: Adapted from Cooper and Slagmulder (2003).

A networked-based approach to management accounting and the design of accounting information networks for collaborative relationships: going a step further

The overview of the management accounting techniques presented so far, and included in the literature, has helped to clarify the use of accounting in collaborating relationships, but it is characterised by two relevant flaws. Firstly, the techniques have been mainly considered at the dyadic level of analysis. For example, open-book accounting has been mainly studied from the perspective of a partnership between only two firms (Håkansson and Lind, 2007), though such approach could be more effective when applied to the entire set of collaborating firms. Also inter-organisational cost accounting techniques, even when referred to many buyer firms and their entire set of suppliers, have been investigated only on selected dyadic relationships (Cooper and Slagmulder, 2004). This focus has not allowed researchers to grasp the complete picture and account for the heterogeneity of accounting practices at the level of the entire network. Secondly, the different contributors have focussed on the mere description of techniques instead of developing and assessing various alternatives, and proposing some principles for designing accounting information exchanges.

One way of overcoming these limitations is to look at the entire set of accounting information flows, taking place between all the collaborating firms, and to discuss the corresponding design implications. In this way, it would be possible to explore the impact that certain accounting information exchanges between two firms have on other firms and/or relationships, and their differential influence on the overall accounting information exchanges. In fact, each network of collaborating firms is a peculiar combination of multiple and multifaceted relationships whose functioning cannot be fully understood by describing the accounting information exchanged by each pair or different pairs of relationships at a time, but rather by considering all the accounting flows as a whole and at the same time. Therefore, the more global and simultaneous is the investigation of such complex nexus of accounting information flows, the more the view becomes comprehensive and the design of such flows, uniquely specified. Considering all the management accounting information flows between all the different collaborating parties at the same time allows to look at these information exchanges as a network. Therefore, we call this comprehensive set of accounting information flows between collaborating firms as *Accounting Information Network (AIN)*. This latter can be defined as a '*multilevel information system aiming at organising, processing and sharing accounting information*' in order to:

- plan a collaborative future by setting down what each party wishes to achieve from the collaboration, how feasible the goals and relative roles are and what actions need to be taken;
- verify that the actions of the other collaborative parties are in accordance with defined goals and expectations;
- support multi-layered decision-making processes' (Amigoni et al., 2003).

The analysis of the network of accounting information permits to investigate its structural properties as a basis for developing design principles. The structural properties refer to specific dimensions, which can be used to direct attention to relevant features of the AIN. Some of these key dimensions are (see Wasserman and Faust, 1994; Soda, 1988):

- *Centralisation*: which refers to the extent to which a firm in the network is quite central with remaining actors considerably less central. These latter might be viewed as residing in the periphery.
- *Density*: which describes the general level of linkage among the firms in a network as the number of connections, expressed as a proportion of the maximum possible number of them.
- *Connectivity*: which is the minimum number of firms whose removal would not allow the network to remain connected or would reduce the

network to but a single member. It measures the level of cohesion of a network at a general level.

These dimensions assume different forms in various contexts and make the circulation of information more efficient and effective, depending, as suggested by the organisational literature, on the governance structure as a result of the characteristics of transactions and the complexity of the task that needs to be carried out (Bavelas, 1951; Freeman et al., 1980; Chapman, 1998).

The governance structure: the transactions undertaken with the counterpart can be regulated either with arm's length principles (market) or with bureaucratic mechanisms (hierarchy). When transactions are market-based none of the parties assumes a prominent role, and the network is organised among peers. In this case, the AIN is decentralised in that there is little variation between the number of information exchanges each firm undertakes. On the contrary, when transactions are hierarchy-based, one or a few firms tend to assume a focal role in the governance of transactions. As a consequence the AIN is centralized around one or a few firms. These latter are more central to the extent they exchange information with more firms within the network, have a higher number of links, and are more tied to non-connected others.

The complexity of the task: this is the result of some of the variables that have been proposed in the previous chapters. When the task generates simply sequential interdependence between parties (one party provides the inputs to the other), the knowledge of the transformation process is high (it is possible to pre-specify all the steps to carry out the task) and the output is easily measurable, the level of complexity is assumed to be low. On the contrary, when the task generates reciprocal interdependence between parties (one party provides the inputs to the other and vice versa), the knowledge of the transformation process is limited (it is not possible to define all the activities to carry out the task in advance and exceptions are frequent) and the output cannot be easily measured, the level of complexity of the task is assumed to be high. One example of the first situation is the task of producing a very standard product (e.g. a t-shirt) as requested by another party. One example of the second situation refers to the case in which two parties collaborate in the task of designing a complex product (e.g. a pair of shoes) and while one party is also in charge of producing the product, the other is responsible for providing materials.

When complexity is low, integration between the various units of the network require AINs with low density and connectivity. In this case, standardised accounting information provides the input for planning future activities, controlling partners and for effectively supporting decision-making processes. On the contrary, when complexity is high, the integration necessary to decide on goals and activities, monitor partners' action and make proper decisions requires that accounting information is embedded in a densely connected web of interactions between the different firms belonging to the network.

The possibility to manage accounting information with different degrees of centrality, density and connectivity derives from the peculiar nature of the AIN's intelligence (Sawhney and Parikh, 2001). In fact, the location of this intelligence can be de-coupled into back-end and front-end. The first type of intelligence, the back-end one, is usually embedded in a shared infrastructure at the network's core. This type of intelligence is, therefore, centralised, robust, scalable and standardised. On the contrary, the second type of intelligence, the front-end one, can be distributed at the network periphery, and is characterised for being decentralised, flexible, personalised and contextualised.

The two types of intelligence have different nature: the first one, is needed for interaction, while the second one, is suitable for processing and storing information. They are complementary but, if de-coupled, they empower each other, since back-end intelligence can be efficiently consolidated in a shared infrastructure so that front-end intelligence, freed from basic processing and storing functions, can be customised according to the needs of any final user (Sawhney and Parikh, 2001). Yet, a complete decoupling can be achieved only in case of low level of complexity. In the other cases, the two types of intelligence cannot be completely de-coupled because the back-end intelligence is shaped according to the specific needs of the front-end intelligence. According to this logic accounting represents a shared standard for information exchange, which enables individual pieces of intelligence to flow and be recombined anywhere along the network (Amigoni et al., 2003).

The multiplicity of levels of an AIN resides in the fact that it acknowledges both the organisational and inter-organisational effects; views decisions as a function of both the cross-organisational shared context and the single units' cognitive processing; allows a dynamic balance for both routinised information collection and problem solving as specified by collective context and ad hoc information gathering done by single units for decision making; permits alternatives to be evaluated at the level of both the whole networked organisation and the single molecular units. The consistency between these various levels is guaranteed by the use of a common language of communication, that is to say the accounting language, which functions as a frame, an integrative structure, providing shared interpretation of events thereby serving two roles: meaning assignment and linking mechanism (Amigoni et al., 2003).

One possible methodology that can be useful in checking up and designing AINs is the mapping of all the flows between the different firms belonging to the network, unveiling in this way patterns of interactions and exchanges of information (Borgatti et al., 1992; Scott, 1991; Tichy et al., 1979). The strength of this methodology is that it concentrates on the overall system of relations (Table 5.1).

The methodology for checking up and designing AINs can be articulated in the following phases:

- identify who belongs to the network (firms and managers involved);
- survey the managers in the network to determine existing connections among them;
- use computer software (e.g. Ucinet) to represent graphically the network;
- interview the key managers of the different firms to explore their information needs;
- identify potential problems and opportunities for improvement in accounting information exchanges through individual meetings and workshops;
- redesign and implement interventions to change the centralisation, density and connectivity of the AIN depending on the characteristics of transactions and tasks;
- follow up and fine-tuning of the interventions;
- map the AIN again after a period of time.

6

'Fashionable' control
and information sharing
practices of collaborating
firms

The last chapter integrates the theoretical considerations with some relevant experiences of collaboration between firms. The empirical evidence reported here is the result of a research project entitled 'Management Accounting in Networks: Techniques and Applications' funded by CIMA. More specifically, we selected the most interesting insights from our investigations mainly referring to: a survey of a sample of management accountants selected from UK (CIMA members) and Italy, and four in-depth case studies on selected fashion firms. The findings are interpreted through the lenses of the concepts and references sketched in the previous chapters. A framework for analysing case studies and providing some guidelines for designing accounting information networks and control systems is presented. The book concludes with some final considerations and recommendations to guide managers in management accounting and control systems implementation.[1]

Contemporary control practices in collaborative relationships: a survey

The data related to the survey were collected by means of a questionnaire. This latter was organised in four sections, aimed at analysing management accounting practices in collaborative relationships.

The first part of the questionnaire was meant to gather general information on the respondents' firms: industry, number of employees, revenues and return on investment (ROI).

The second part of the questionnaire comprised questions related to the features of the partners with which the respondents' firms entertain collaborative activities. Questions had the objective of assessing the relevance of each partners' category. Specific questions were asked about the type of contractual agreement (i.e. agency contract, licensing, franchising, joint venture, etc.).

In addition, the benefits deriving from the collaboration with the partners were investigated (i.e. cost reductions, inventory reductions, quality and service improvement, faster response to market, etc.).

The third part concentrated on the characteristics of the relationship such as the level of asset specificity (plants, IT, competencies) and the duration of the relationship to understand the appropriate and likely mechanisms of regulating transactions (market vs hierarchy based).

---

[1] We want to acknowledge the contribution of Anisa Shyti in writing up this chapter.

Table 6.1 Revenues of the respondents.

	Per cent	Cumulative per cent
Not valid	11.1	11.1
<1 million £	2.8	13.9
1–2.9 million £	16.7	30.6
5–7.4 million £	11.1	41.7
7.5–24.9 million £	11.1	52.8
25–49.9 million £	11.1	63.9
50–99.9 million £	11.1	75.0
100–199.9 million £	2.8	77.8
>200 million £	22.2	100.0
Total	100.0	

The last and fourth part was dedicated to the analysis of management accounting and control practices adopted to regulate exchanges between the firms and their partners. Elements that were investigated referred to the partners' participation in control processes, strategic planning, budgeting, the performance measurement, evaluation and reward of partners and the degree of reciprocal knowledge between partners. Specific questions were directed at exploring the type of management accounting information exchanged between partners. Some final questions were also asked on the role of management accountants in the governance of the relationships.

In the questions we adopted a 7-point Likert scale going from 1 – not at all to 7 – to a very great extent as well as yes or no responses and priority lists.

General characteristics of collaborating partners (Chapter 1)

The respondents' firms mainly belong to services (19.3%), manufacturing (16.7%), oil and chemical (13.9%), health care and social assistance (8.3%), and finance and insurance (8.3%). All the other industries are almost equally represented.

To get some general information on the size of the investigated companies we collected some data on revenues and ROI (see Tables 6.1 and 6.2).

One of the questions required the respondents to specify the three main collaborating partners. The objective was to identify the range of potential partners of the respondents' firms. The table reported here (Table 6.3) indicates the number of times each type of partner was mentioned by the firms.

Table 6.2 ROI of the respondents.

	Per cent	Cumulative per cent
Not valid	41.7	41.7
<0%	2.8	44.5
0–4%	8.3	52.8
5–9%	16.7	69.5
10–14%	11.1	80.6
25–29%	2.8	83.4
35–39%	8.3	91.7
>40%	8.3	100
Total	100.0	

Table 6.3 The firms' most relevant partners.

	Per cent
Raw material supplier	22.2
Work in progress	5.6
Specialised manufacturer	33.3
Wholesaler	22.2
Retailer	22.2
Internal logistics	5.6
Transport	13.9
Post sales support	8.3
Other	33.3

Data suggest that the three more relevant partners for the firms under investigation are: the specialised manufacturers, the raw materials suppliers, and the wholesalers and retailers.

Most firms rely on formal contracts to regulate the relationships with partners (see Figure 6.1). More specifically, the most represented are: agency contracts (27.8%), outsourcing agreements (27.8%) and joint ventures arrangements (11.1%).

Reasons for collaboration (Chapter 2)

A constant and powerful reason that triggers interorganisational collaboration is the possibility to achieve some reciprocal economic advantages linked to

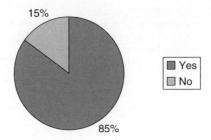

Figure 6.1 Existence of a formal contract

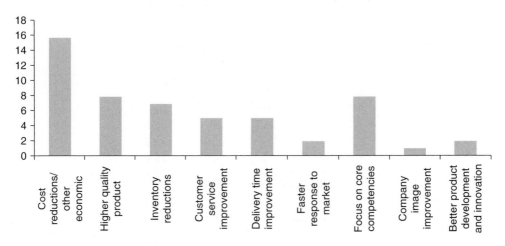

Figure 6.2 Reasons for collaboration

cost reduction. Other important advantages are related to improvement of the quality of products and the need to refocus on core competencies (Figure 6.2).

Governance structure (Chapter 3)

Some further questions were directed to understanding the characteristics of partners in terms of investments made specifically for the management relationship. Particularly significant in this respect is to notice that asset specificity is a relevant feature in many cases (41%) (see Figure 6.3).

With reference to asset specificity different respondents stressed the relevance of different investment categories. For each category respondents

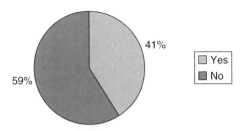

Figure 6.3 Existence of specific investments to sustain the relationship

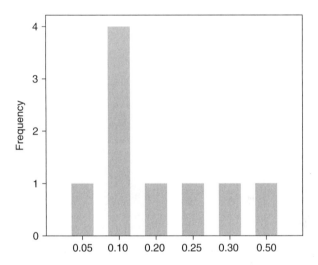

Figure 6.4 Investments in plants specific to the collaboration

were required to indicate this relevance with reference to total investments (for plants and IT) and to total working time (for training) (Figures 6.4–6.6).

Another aspect that was investigated in the questionnaire was related to the duration of the collaborations. The relationships with these partners have lasted on average 9 years (see Figure 6.7).

These two aspects of the collaboration are used to proxy the nature of the relationships and show whether they are more market or more hierarchy based. This is because a high investment in assets and long lasting, repeated transactions lead to the adoption of more bureaucratic mechanism of management.

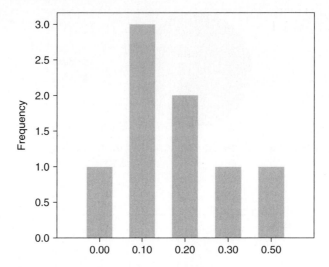

Figure 6.5   Investments in IT specific to the collaboration

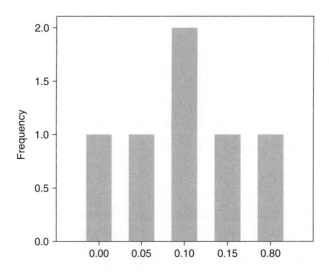

Figure 6.6   Investments in training specific to the collaboration

Control modes (Chapter 4)

With reference to managerial processes, some firms (13.9%) declared that their most important partners participate in their control processes. This kind of control is exercised on the one hand with direct inspections at the

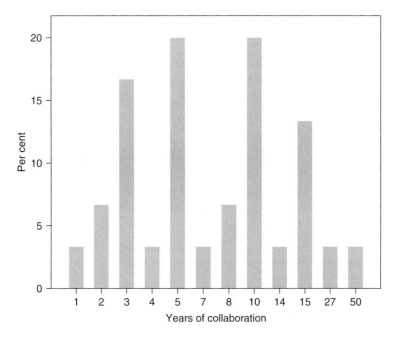

Figure 6.7   The duration of the collaboration with the most important partner

partners' sites and, on the other hand, with a direct involvement and monitoring of operations (see Figures 6.8 and 6.9).

Collaborative planning, performance measurement, cost and other management accounting information exchanges (Chapter 5)

The analysed firms that declared their critical partners participate to a great extent in their strategic planning are 8.4% and in the budgeting process are 13.9%.

In relation to performance measurement and evaluation, 66.7% of the surveyed firms affirmed that they regularly assess the results of their partners mainly through: quality indicators (41.7%), customer satisfaction indicators (38.9%), delivery and time indicators (36.1%) and financial indicators (25%) (see Figure 6.10). In addition, 30.6% of these firms use incentive systems to reward their partners.

As the findings indicate that the respondents' firms have a deeper understanding of the operating activities of their partners (see Figure 6.11) than

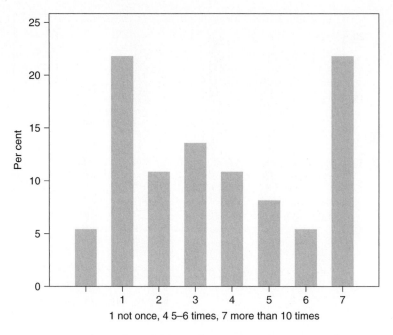

Figure 6.8 Process control: number of visits to the partners' sites in a month

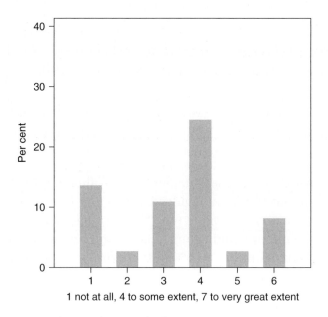

Figure 6.9 Process control: operations monitoring

Figure 6.10 Performance measurement indicators

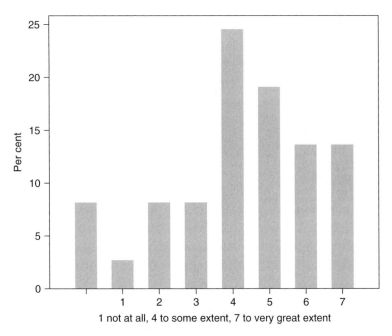

1 not at all, 4 to some extent, 7 to very great extent

Figure 6.11 The respondents firms' knowledge of the operations of the partners

these latter have of the former (see Figure 6.12) this might suggest the preva-
lent role of a focal firm.

Concerning the information that respondents exchange more frequently with
their partners the following table provides a summary, indicating a certain

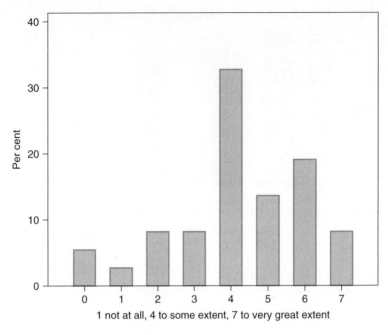

Figure 6.12   The partners' knowledge of the operations of the respondents firms

prevalence of non-financial management accounting information, and of actual ones (see Table 6.4).

Finally, the questionnaire investigated the role of management accountants. Respondents reported that management accountants intervene to great extent in the coordination of financial information exchanges with their most important partners in 22.2% of the cases and in non-financial information exchanges in 16.7% of the firms analysed.

The data collected with the survey lead us to draw some conclusions on the type of relationships that the firms in the sample undertake with their collaborating partners, and on the way of regulating the corresponding transactions with the use of management accounting.[2] While these conclusions are simply descriptive of the sample under investigation and cannot be generalised, they however provide an interesting overview of the potential ways that firms can adopt to manage collaboration.

---

[2] Note that for the analysis and interpretation of data we referred to Lorenzoni and Baden-Fuller (1995) and De Wit and Meyer (2004).

Table 6.4 Information exchanges between collaborating partners.

Financial information	Actual (%)	Forecasted (%)
Revenues	22	
Revenues per customer	11	17
Raw material costs	25	11
Labour costs	19	11
Depreciation	17	
Other indirect manufacturing costs	14	11
Cost of goods sold	19	11
R&D expenses	11	
SG&A expenses	11	
Produt margin	17	
Liquidity	11	
Non-financial information	**Actual (%)**	**Forecasted (%)**
Cycle time/lead time	17	
Development speed/time to market	17	
On time delivery/delay	36	
Storage time	11	
Production volume	17	
Volume and order mix	14	11
Goods sold out	19	14
Productivity	14	
Inventory turns	11	
Returns (for defects)	25	
Reworks	17	
Spoilage	11	
New product sales	11	14
New product vs competitors	11	
Complaints	22	
Repeat sales	17	

First of all, data suggest that while firms have relationships of different sorts, firms seem to concentrate their collaboration efforts over upstream (supplier) relations and downstream (buyer) relations. These upstream relations refer to collaboration with providers of materials, work in progress and services. In a wider sense they include also the collaboration with the providers of every type of resource, be it labour, technology and so on. They can either be the actual producers of the inputs, or intermediaries acting as agents in charge of distributing the product or service. In addition, together with first-tier suppliers, they can also be suppliers positioned further upstream in the chain. The downstream relationships refer to connections with intermediaries in charge of selling the object of the transactions. Less common seem to be the downstream relations with the actual users of the product or services and other actors downstream the chain. On the contrary, direct or indirect horizontal collaborative relations (actual or potential competitors) did not emerge in our data. Respondents did not emphasise forms of collaboration with firms that produce similar products or provide equal services, with producers of complementary goods or services, with potential industry entrants or with firms in other industries.

Secondly, data suggest that among all the different forms of collaborative arrangements that firms can use to structure their links with one another the contractual form seems to be privileged. This means that collaboration is often assisted by legal enforceability, while financial stake in each other (equity-based arrangements) and the use of social/informal connections (non-contractual arrangements) seem to be less common. The use of these contractual forms seem to indicate that the firms investigated try to combine the benefits of the market with those of the hierarchy. They attempt to retain the flexibility and motivation of the former, and the convergence of goals and coordination of activities of the latter. By avoiding to be completely locked into a fixed hierarchy, they can activate multiple relations characterised by various levels of length and intensity, being facilitated in this way in adaptation when circumstances require change.

Thirdly, with reference to the objectives of collaboration, data suggest that firms in the sample undertake mainly relations aimed at integrating activities. As it is difficult for them to span an entire value chain from top to bottom and excel in each phase of the total process, they integrate their value chains with other firms, being in this way more efficient and effective than if they were completely autonomous. They activate collaboration, both upstream and downstream, because they want to concentrate on only certain value-adding processes, but need different inputs as well as various channels for distributing their products or services. In contrast, in the sample, firms did not indicate collaboration for sharing operations, sales infrastructures or accounting facilities to achieve economies of scale. In addition, none of the firm referred to collaboration aimed at leveraging resources (lending resources that one cannot make full use of) or aligning positions (combining bargaining powers to strengthen each other position).

Fourthly, the evidence collected emphasise a particular nature of the relationships between the collaborating firms. The relevance of asset specificity, the frequency of interaction and the expectation of future interactions (9 years is the average length of the relationships) suggest situations of reciprocal and tight dependence among parties which make these relationships resemble those of the hierarchy. They are characterised by the joint use of their resources and the common execution of activities. However, this dependence is unbalanced, as suggested by the fact that firms declare they have a deeper understanding of the operating activities of their partners than these latter have of the former. This means that one party dominates the other and has more freedom to manoeuvre and impose its conditions to the counterpart. It acts as a strategic centre that outsources and shares with more partners than the traditional firm and that coordinates partners and defines their roles in a positive and creative way in order to make the whole system function.

Finally, the data indicate participation of partners in the planning, budgeting and control processes of the firms, and the exchange of financial and non-financial management accounting information, being the latter predominant. This suggests that the collaborating firms that specialise in a particular function have access to others in the systems performing complementary tasks and this creates a level playing field within the network. Original modes of exchanging information may lead to new ways of doing business together, providing a source of competitive advantage. The availability of information on many aspects of the business facilitates more rapid responses to market opportunities. In contrast, the firms of the sample did not indicate that the sharing of management accounting information led to adversarial consequences (83.4 of the respondents), like for example the use of shared information for one's own advantage, without reciprocating, the exploitation to create superior bargaining positions, or, finally, in extreme situations, the utilisation of shared information to activate a rival collaboration to the detriment of the original information provider.

As a whole, data seem to suggest that collaborating partners activate networks in which a firm plays a central role in coordinating the activities of the counterparts and designs a network structure (the Accounting Information Network) that provides an environment favourable for information to be generated and exchanged. The information exchanged in the network seems to be 'thicker' than that condensed through the brokerage market, but is 'freer' than that in the hierarchy.

Multiple case study analysis: comparing control practices in partnerships

The in-depth case studies were conducted with reference to renowned, international fashion firms. Due to confidentiality reasons, we cannot disclose the names of the firms under study.

We analysed the firms over 12 months. Data were collected with in-depth interviews with senior managers, controllers, information system managers and selected operational managers. The check list of the interviews comprised a series of questions with the objective of deepening our understanding not only of the accounting and control practices in use but also of the variables that influence them.

Data were also collected by means of archival sources – financial statements, corporate publications and other written material. In the selection of the respondents we paid attention to address different levels of responsibility and seniority to get a broad and varied picture of the phenomenon under study. The questions were open and on average the interviews lasted 3 h. Follow-ups were also carried out to focus on specific issues, reconcile different interpretations and integrate the findings.

In the firms' investigation, we followed some common steps throughout the cases: firstly, we focused on a company overview and on the relationships between the firms and its partners in order to explore the nature of the underlying agreements. The goal was to outline the managerial practices used by these firms to sustain their collaborative relationships. Secondly, we devoted our attention to the specific governance and control structure, the collaborative planning, the performance measurement systems and the inter-firm cost and other information exchanges between partners. Finally, we investigated the specific contextual variables (e.g. type of interdependencies, knowledge of the transformation process, output measurability, and so on) that affect management accounting and control practices.

A particular attention was given to issues of comparison between different sites both when collecting data and when elaborating them. For this purpose, with reference to each case, we provide a table that summarises and highlights the main managerial issues and variables described throughout this book:

(1) Counterparts' presentation and reasons for collaboration (Chapters 1 and 2).

(2) Governance structure (Chapter 3).
(3) Forms of control and their determinants (Chapter 4).
(4) Collaborative planning, performance measurement, cost and other management accounting information exchanges (Chapter 5).

Evidence from *FirmA*

Company overview

FirmA is the operating holding company of a group that develops, manufactures, promotes and distributes footwear and apparel characterised by the application of innovative and technological solutions.

FirmA manufactures classic, casual and sport footwear for men, women and kids within the medium to medium-high price range. Recently, the firm launched a clothing collection, mainly sportswear, for men and women. The *FirmA* brand is therefore a family brand that offers a wide range of products, each of which is characterised by innovation, comfort and a style that is in line with the latest fashion trends.

FirmA is considered a leader in the national and international classical and casual footwear market. In 2004, around 45% of consolidated revenues in the footwear sector were achieved on some main foreign markets, including Germany, France, Spain and USA.

In 2004, *FirmA*'s sales were 340 million euro, its operating income was 70 million euro and its ROI was equal to 25%.

Business model

One of *FirmA*'s strength is its supply chain organisation. Its main feature is the flexibility of the business model and its decentralisation. *FirmA* operates in outsourcing and is able to manage the production and logistic cycles effectively while achieving tough control over the critical phases of the value chain. The production processes are also largely delocalised. Both outsourced and delocalised processes are centrally managed by *FirmA* headquarters.

The actors of the network
The actors of the network are:

- raw leather suppliers;
- directly owned subsidiaries;

- third-party manufacturing companies, in charge of specific non-leather products;
- mono and multi-brands shops, both owned and in franchising.

The internal manufacturing processes take mainly place in two factories owned by *FirmA* located in Eastern Europe. These plants produce around 20% of the total production. The remaining 80% is produced by third parties' factories, mainly in Asia and South America.

Unlike most Asian and South American factories, the two European sites can manufacture a whole leather shoe. Costs are higher in the eastern European plants, but the workforce has the know-how to manufacture many different styles. Nonetheless *FirmA*, like most other manufacturers, cannot avoid outsourcing to Asia and South America and it has people scouting around the world all the time. They outsource the production of products, not the single production phases.

To maintain a tight control over the outsourced processes, there is a specific company that has been created in order to oversee *FirmA's* manufacturing activities. The company also purchases raw materials from selected suppliers, mainly in the headquarters' country, in order to guarantee the highest quality standards, both at the directly owned production plants and at third producers' sites. This company uses its own technical staff to coordinate plant production activities and to assess the quality of the finished goods.

For what concerns distribution, there is a network of mono-brand shops and other multi-brand shops, on the basis of the distribution structure of each country. *FirmA's* products are sold in over 68 countries worldwide through a widespread distribution network of more than 250 single-brand stores and about 8,000 multi-brand sales points. This network includes both directly owned and franchising shops. The goal of the distributing network is to optimise the commercial penetration into the single markets and to promote the *FirmA* brand consistently to all end consumers.

The distribution and commercial activities are controlled by *FirmA* through different subsidiaries, which are held accountable of sales points and marketing for the country of reference. Moreover, each company provides customer service to the parent company and controls the sales network in the country location. These subsidiaries are very important in the rapidly expanding markets for managing and developing the network of franchisees and for employing new staff for the sales force.

The process

All the critical phases of the manufacturing process are closely monitored by *FirmA* as well as the sourcing of raw materials and the product development. *FirmA* selects third-party producers with great accuracy, considering the technical competences of the partner company, its quality standards and its capacity to cope with the production volumes within the tight deadlines. Interestingly, *FirmA* has adopted a specific technology, now widespread among Europe's leading fashion retailers, which rapidly provides headquarters with information about which shoe styles are selling at which stores, so that production can be adjusted accordingly. In this fast-paced environment, the fact that shoes produced in Eastern Europe reach the store shelves overnight in the main markets of the firm, compared with the 30 days by sea from Asia, is a big advantage.

The finished goods from all the production plants are subsequently consolidated at *FirmA*'s distribution centres situated at the headquarters.

In each plant there are the *FirmA* technicians continuously controlling the whole production process and ready to stop it if something is not as it should be. In addition, each pair of shoes goes back to the headquarters to be stocked. Only in this way *FirmA* can control toughly the quality of its products.

At the end of the production cycle, the finished goods undergo quality tests and if they pass, they are packed and sent to the headquarters, to be distributed to stores and mono-brand shops.

Control and accounting issues: the findings

In this section, contents and quotes from open-ended interviews undertaken with some key actors of *FirmA* are reported, in order to present how the relationships among the different parties operating within the *FirmA* network are regulated. The purpose is to describe the role of management accounting and control mechanisms underlying the different collaborative relationships.

To give a thorough view of the findings, some important strings of the interview will be reported and commented by taking as a reference some of the concepts illustrated in the previous chapters, i.e. the governance and control structure (Chapters 3 and 4), performance, costing and collaborative programming issues (Chapter 5).

The governance and control structure

Basically, *FirmA* has reproduced its own model abroad, creating a centrally coordinated manufacturing network. On the one side, this network, by leveraging on independent third-party manufacturers, is very reactive and flexible. On the other side, though processes have been largely delocalised and outsourced, quality and conformance are guaranteed by the strict controls carried out both by the directly owned coordinating companies and by the technical staff at *FirmA* headquarters. The governance model is the one of a hierarchical type of network, characterised by a high level of asset specificity due to brand-name capital (from which the importance of quality controls at different stages of the value chain) and high frequency and uncertainty of transactions (due to the fast changing requirements imposed especially on production to take into account the market demand trends).

More specifically, the *FirmA* controller said:

> 'We have a very flexible business model, which permits us a prompt organisation of all activities. This is the most important asset we have at *FirmA*, of course after the ideas and after our technology. Each outsourced phase or process is strictly monitored by *FirmA* staff and employees. This is the only way to warrant the quality our customers deserve'.

Regarding the activities that have been outsourced the controller continued:

> 'About the prototyping and other development activities these are managed centrally by *FirmA*, for the lines manufactured internally, in *FirmA* plants in Europe. For what concerns the outsourced production, we provide our suppliers of finished goods with key technical information regarding the features of the product and they develop every step autonomously'.

He also explained the criteria according to which activities are outsourced:

> 'This decision depends upon the kind of product. Products with rubber soles, plastic or technical tissue, are manufactured in China, being the Chinese plants very well equipped, even in terms of technology. Other kinds of products, such as leather shoes, require a different know-how, that Chinese factories do not possess. So far, this kind of manufacturing is performed only in *FirmA*'s owned factories, mainly located in Europe. Summarising, we can assume that in most cases the choice is made on the kind of product and its features'.

To avoid problems in later phases of manufacturing, *FirmA* pays particular attention to the partner selection process. They base their evaluation on previous experience or on certifiable elements, as explained by the chief operating officer:

> 'There is a careful selection of the future partners. For the time being, there is not a formal certifying procedure. The evaluation and assessment of the parties is based on visits of *FirmA* experts and engineers to the plants during the production, interviews, and so forth. Then we take into account public sources of information, as the image of the company, previous experience, capabilities of its employers'.

As previously mentioned, in *FirmA* the raw material selection and processing is extremely important, in order to guarantee the quality of the finished product. *FirmA* is involved in the early phases of hides purchasing and processing. Though some relationships are held with the cattle breeders in their specific markets, most leather is bought in the headquarters' country. *FirmA*'s aim is to control all phases regarding the shoe leather supplying, so it has all information regarding the prices, the quality, the yield rate of each kind of leather.

On the selection of raw materials, the controller further stated that:

> 'Generally, we have a structured supplying process. So we acquire the shoe leather as hides, in a very raw state and we process it in our laboratories, or in the laboratories of some third related parties. Control is very strict in this phase, as the volume produced is pretty high. Frequently, the purchasing process in this phase can be managed through auctions or negotiations on the raw shoe leather. Of course there is a big effort to manage the relationship with the suppliers, which in many cases is well built through time'.

As explained by the controller, this choice is motivated not only by the economies of scale but also, and especially, by the high quality of leather *FirmA* wants to maintain independently from where the shoes are produced. In fact, to maintain its brand reputation, *FirmA* has to provide to the customers an excellent product. For this reason, controls over the collaborating parties occur in different phases of the manufacturing process. These controls are performed directly by *FirmA* experts on the third parties plants. Controls are performed both before the delivery of the finished goods to *FirmA* warehouses, and, afterwards, through a random control on the delivered batches.

Collaborative planning

The company is able to autonomously evaluate the impact of including some external parties into the production process when defining the budget. As the controller explained:

'Since production activities, both internal and outsourced ones, are managed in a very centralised fashion, we have a production plan, done by our headquarters' control function, including all production, both internal and external [...] This is also done because our third-party manufacturers are not sole suppliers. So we need to program and schedule both internal and outside production to "book" in advance their production capacity'.

Programming the production requires also including the constraints of the distributors, as orders come from them. In fact:

'The production gets initiated on the basis of the general manager and of the marketing manager's projections [...] As orders get progressively collected from wholesalers and owned-stores, we need to revise these projections to manufacture just the products that we need to produce given the requests of the market. This means that we need then to go back to our third-party manufacturers to adjust the production mix and allocation'.

Performance measurement

The performance drivers in this company are referred to production cost items. The profitability depends on *FirmA* capability to meet the target costs:

'It is the sales budget that is our engine. More specifically, the target margins and the target costs, the discussions with our third-parties, our internal analysis lead to a definition of prices... obviously, it is the market that makes the prices but we want to understand what is the amount of the contribution we can get from each product to cover our fixed costs and be profitable. Our attention is focused on the product costs and on production overhead. We pay a lot of attention to the definition of a target cost'.

That is the reason why production variance analysis is fundamental in *FirmA* for performance measurement and management. They calculate, as clarified by the controller, the traditional price and efficiency variances.

Regarding external relationships with manufacturing partners, since these relationships are rather long term ones and information about third parties have been collected through time, *FirmA* is fairly competent to assess also the performance, in terms of productivity and profitability, of each of its collaborators.

More specifically, regarding the information required from the manufacturing network actors:

'Each product has a specific datasheet supplying information on manufacturing parameters, yield rates, efficiency rates, cutting, etc. Obviously working with leather presents some difficulties, as it is not a specified, precisely quantifiable material. You have different pieces, different dimensions, different colours, and different smoothness. So it depends enormously on the skills and capacities of the craftsmen that manage the laboratory [...] The scratch level depends on the raw leather quality, on the cutter's ability, and so forth. There are many factors. The most important thing is that we provide to our collaborators some parameters, consumption rates, yield rates, to have a benchmark on the usage. All these data represent average consumption rates, and do not include any extraordinary events. So, if the manufacturer incurs higher consumption of materials this is not *FirmA*'s concern. Instead, if there were any problem regarding the quality of the processed leather, an inverse interactive cycle with the manufacturer to establish the causes and the responsibilities is activated'.

As explained by the chief operating officer (COO), *FirmA*'s manufacturing partners buy the leather and the other raw materials from *FirmA* and proceed with the assembling phase or other manufacturing phases. In such situations, the firm is not any more responsible for the efficiency of the suppliers, as in cases of higher consumption rates, they have to ask *FirmA* and pay for additional raw material supply, as by contract.

'Being the leather a scarce resource, we have very tight manufacturing times. Moreover, the fashion world has these characteristics regarding the timing. In cases of inefficiency, there is a process of investigation, if the problem is harmful to *FirmA*'s image. In other cases, when conditions are previously defined on a contractual basis, we just apply the rule'.

For what concerns the reliability of information to evaluate performance and trust, the controller further commented:

'Of course there is some trust. How can you build relationships without trust? And in the long-term relationships we trust our collaborators. Even though, there are some *FirmA* employees in loco, just to help both sides. We know the average parameters on which to benchmark the performance of the factory. Problems usually arise on the timing, as in cases of delays, but we can manage this'.

At a more consolidated level, for performance evaluation, *FirmA* defines different income statements, both budgeted and actual, by store, by distribution channel, by region, by product and by customer typology (women, men and kids). *FirmA* does not define any income statement by collection. While by region and by distribution channel, the calculation of margins is pushed till the net income, with reference to the store and to the customer dimension it is the revenues that are the main focus to control for performance.

Costing issues

The following items are included in the calculation of unitary product costs:

- Direct materials;
- Direct labour;
- Indirect materials;
- Custom duties;
- Transportation costs.

Production overhead are not the focus of product costs analysis even though they pay particular attention to the ROI related to dies:

'Instead of allocating depreciation costs on the product units, we try to understand whether our production volumes can sustain and justify the investment in a specific die'.

Regarding the definition of the production cost of external parties for use in negotiation, the controller commented:

'The detail and depth of our analysis on our external parties costs depend on the knowledge of the production process and of the technology possessed by each supplier. When we deal with highly skilled and un-substitutable counterparts producing very specific products, we define a target cost through an independent technical analysis of the products' characteristics and then we use it for negotiating the single cost items with the supplier, to reach a certain target margin. For other products, the most standard ones, there is a price that is determined by the market. With the suppliers of these products we negotiate only the commercial conditions (time, volumes...)'.

With reference to highly skilled and un-substitutable suppliers, also some indirect costs are included in the definition of the acquisition price, as illustrated by the controller:

'We recognise them a higher price for the design and development of products. This can be included as a percentage of the production cost (a mark up) or negotiated as a lump-sum not included in the unitary production cost. Basically, in this last case, it is like paying them for a consulting activity'.

Interestingly, for those third-party manufacturers for which *FirmA* defines a target cost, the controller performs variance analysis, carried on in the same way of the one for internal activities, and on the basis of technical standard defined by *FirmA*.

Cost and other management accounting exchanges

FirmA is making progress towards building a flexible integrated IT system, organised as a network, which will enable the firm to face the future challenges represented by significant increase in buying, outsourcing and selling.

As explained by the controller:

'The manufacturing process is managed centrally by *FirmA*. We achieve control thanks to the information exchanges during each phase of manufacturing. Of course, *FirmA* expertise on the single phases is very important to select what kind of information to collect. Even though, we cannot always rely on direct control, especially regarding the factories in the Far East, which are not *FirmA* exclusive. In these cases we can rely on remote control. This is made possible thanks to our information technology system that allows us to collect information in real time. Information is about the advancement of the production, work in progress activities, follow-up phases, and so forth'.

Also stores are connected through the IT system to the headquarters:

'We know what they sell and how much they sell. Also with reference to franchising stores'.

The controller further explained that having a unique IT system brings some advantages in terms of synchronisation of activities, homogenisation of languages, techniques and methodologies.

'We share our methodologies, we have standardised them. We have created a common datawarehouse while formerly we did everything on excel. When we used customised excel sheets, the data had some problems of coherence...'

FirmA situation regarding its interorganisational relationships is characterised by high interdependence. The firm sells technology and innovative ideas, and its partners provide it with high quality finished goods.

To make the process work, *FirmA* has to control each phase, from the raw material selection to distribution. *FirmA* selects its collaborating partners carefully, in order to rely on long-term relationships. Long term means trust development, reliability on skills and capabilities of craftsmen, reliability on financial and non-financial exchanged information.

Contracts that support these relationships are designed to allow frequent interactions, reciprocal knowledge, know-how transfer, without being harmful to the parties.

FirmA is the central actor of its network and the relationships system on which it relies assures control and reliable information. This is obvious from the fact that *FirmA* expansion was a consequence of natural growth, responding positively to market's needs. Its growth was not driven by mergers or acquisitions. This explain why *FirmA* aimed at establishing closer relations with its collaborators than normal arm's length relations.

Table 6.5 summarises the characteristics of the external relationships of *FirmA* with its different counterparts and reports the specifics of management control patterns and accounting information exchanges.

Evidence from *FirmB*

Company overview

FirmB is one of the most well-known world players in the clothing apparel industry. It is present world-wide in more than 100 countries and produces around 130 million garments every year. In particular, *FirmB* manufactures and sells garments in yarns and in fabrics of wool, cotton, denim and any other natural or synthetic fibre. The firm is also involved in the manufacturing and distribution of accessories and other fashion articles for casual and home wear, and the manufacturing, marketing and distribution of footwear, cosmetics, eyewear, watches, stationery, bags, umbrellas, games and toys.

FirmB operates into three distinct business segments:

(1) Casual wear (including complementary products such as accessories and footwear);
(2) Sportswear and equipment;
(3) Manufacturing and other, including mainly sales of raw materials, semi-finished products, and industrial and advertising services.

FirmB's revenues in 2004 accounted for 1,700 million euro, income from operations for 215 million euro and ROI was 7%.

Table 6.5 Findings on *FirmA*.

Variables and issues	Partners			
	Raw leather suppliers	Subsidiaries	Third independent parties	Commercial network
Description of the counter parts	Independent hides traders that collaborate with *FirmA* on a long-term basis	Equity owned subsidiaries, mainly in Europe, responsible either for manufacturing processes (production companies) or for managing the national sale network (distribution and marketing companies)	Partner firms, which are mainly responsible for manufacturing single products or product types	Mono and multi-brands stores, both owned and franchised
Relationship life cycle	Long, mature relationships	Long, mature relationships	Long, mature relationships	Long, mature relationships
Reasons for collaboration	Quality (importance of raw materials for brand reputation) Efficiency (centralised purchases to leverage on economies of scale)	Quick time-to-market and customisation of customer relationship management	Flexibility and adaptability	Reputation (for owned stores) High competition and efficiency (for franchising stores)
Governance structure	Market-based pattern	Hierarchical relationships (based on equity ownership)	Hierarchical to trust-based pattern	Hierarchical relationships (for owned stores) Contractual relationships, quite hierarchically based (for franchising stores)

(continued)

Table 6.5 (continued).

Variables and issues	Partners			
	Raw leather suppliers	Subsidiaries	Third independent parties	Commercial network
Interdependencies	For closer relations, with continuous interaction, there are likely to be interdependencies related to procedures that have been developed over time. For relationships characterised by a high turnover (the minority) there are not any essential interdependencies	Sequential interdependencies	High sequential interdependence	Sequential interdependence
Knowledge on the transformation process	Medium (processing can lead to different quality leather)	High for the production subsidiaries Medium for the commercial ones	High for standard products Low for products that require highly skilled and un-substitutable suppliers	Medium to low (there is a certain customisation of the selling process depending on the country)
Output measurability	Measures are focused on quality standards	High output measurability both in financial and non-financial terms	High output measurability both in financial and non-financial terms	High output measurability both in financial and non-financial terms

Table 6.5 (continued).

Variables and issues	Partners			
	Raw leather suppliers	Subsidiaries	Third independent parties	Commercial network
Forms of control	Prevalence of output and behaviour control, based on past experience	Prevalence of output control (based on planning and pre-specified performance targets) and social control (staff training)	Prevalence of output and behaviour control (e.g. inspections by technical staff)	Output and input control (for the franchisees) Output control (for the owned shops)
Performance measurement	Quality indicators and productivity indicators	Variances analysis, quality indicators, productivity indicators, waste indicators, time (cycle time, delivery time) indicators	Waste/efficiency indicators, on which the parties are held responsible	Revenues and sales mix
Inter-organisational cost management practices (IOCM)	No IOCM, price is determined on auction or negotiation basis	Traditional cost control practices (variance analysis) Target cost	Traditional cost control practices (variance analysis)Target cost	Not relevant
Cost and management accounting information exchanges	Based on price, quality and process specifications	Information exchange focus on financial and non financial data. On the financial side, they exchange costs, prices, and operating margins. On the other side, data are mostly about operating processes (defect rates, spoilage, cycle time, and so on). Information exchanges are determined by *FirmA* policies	Information exchanges, except for costs, regard mostly non financial items: quantities, cycle time, spoilage, and defect rates	Information exchanges are on revenue items

(continued)

Table 6.5 (continued).

Variables and issues	Partners			
	Raw leather suppliers	Subsidiaries	Third independent parties	Commercial network
Inter-firm information systems	No IT support	Subsidiaries are integrated through an inter-organisational IT system and have reciprocal access to information	The inter-firm information systems is web based and allows parties to access several information types: work in progress, productive capacity	All stores are connected through the IT system and it is possible to collect in real-time information on revenues and types of products sold
The role of management accounting (MA)	Not relevant	MA has a significant role for coordinating and controlling activities	MA has an important role in coordinating and controlling all phases performed by third parties and for defining the responsibilities of exceptions. It also have an important role in programming the allocation of production among the different partners	MA has an important role in coordinating and controlling the network of sales points and for re-forecasting production activities on the basis of actual sales

FirmB tremendous growth, outstanding financial performance and innovative strategies have been captivating the press, the scholars and the practitioners around the world over the past decade.

Business model

There are several factors of *FirmB*'s business model that contributed to its success. First, its innovative operations-management techniques. *FirmB* postpones the garment completion for as long as possible so that decisions about its features can better reflect market trends. Second, the *FirmB*'s manufacturing network, consisting of mainly small and midsize subcontractors, is a critical factor. This structure has contributed to lowering *FirmB*'s manufacturing and labour costs, has reduced its operating risk, shifting it to its suppliers, and has given it high flexibility. Third, the *FirmB*'s distribution network, formed by agents, each responsible for a given market area. *FirmB* does not own the majority of stores; its agents set up a contract relationship, a licensing agreement similar to a franchise, with the store owners, who then sell the products of *FirmB*. This latter, in turn, supports the retailers with several commercial services, such as merchandising.

The actors of the network

The actors of the network are:

- textile and yarn suppliers, controlled through equity ownership;
- foreign manufacturing subsidiaries, totally or partially owned;
- local, small and midsize subcontractors, in charge of labour intensive production phases;
- stores with franchising agreements and owned stores.

Most of *FirmB*'s competitors are international retailers with basically no in-house operations. Also *FirmB*'s manufacturing process is primarily based on outsourcing, basically for the labour intensive production phases, such as tailoring, finishing and ironing. Such phases are outsourced to local small- and medium-sized enterprises. However, the firm keeps in-house strategic activities and operations that require heavy investments, such as weaving, cutting, dyeing, quality control on inputs and on finished goods, quality control on intermediate phases of production. The main factory owned by *FirmB* is a high-tech facility and one the most advanced production sites in the apparel industry. Overseas, *FirmB* has reproduced this model of production by creating foreign manufacturing poles, which are subsidiaries of *FirmB*, totally or partially owned and directly managed by the firm itself (usually ex-*FirmB*'s managers are in charge of these subsidiaries). These production poles manufacture to order. The main factory chooses what should be produced by each of the foreign manufacturers, which then independently decide how to allocate the production tasks among their manufacturing networks. To ensure high quality, the foreign production poles, focus on one type of product and use skills already existing in the area. In the meantime, *FirmB* takes advantage of cost differentials, in particular, of those related to labour.

Recently, the main production pole has transferred to subsidiaries several activities that used to keep in-house, such as quality control on inputs and finished goods, cutting and dyeing. However, it has retained the elaboration, composition and development of the maker sheets for the computerised fabric-cutting system, which are then sent electronically to the foreign manufacturing poles. It also focuses on cutting out prototypes and on quality control of intermediate phases. The main pole and the other foreign production poles can coordinate operations in order to reduce cycle/lead times, through IT and faster communication.

Since in the apparel industry time compression does not depend so much on the tailoring phase as on the supply of raw materials, *FirmB* has gradually increased upstream vertical integration to consolidate its textile and yarn suppliers. Today *FirmB* controls its major supplier of raw materials by a majority of equity ownership.

The distribution network of *FirmB* is composed mainly of mono-brand stores related to the firm through franchising contracts. Such network of independent partners is based on a consolidated entrepreneurial system. The role and value of the partner-entrepreneur system is central to *FirmB*'s strategy aiming to achieve greater competitiveness and flexibility in terms of pricing and margins.

The main constrain for the franchisees is related to the fact that they are bounded to *FirmB* by exclusive contracts. Besides, the prices of products are defined by *FirmB* in order to avoid competitive biddings from franchisees located in the same areas. Also the lay out of the stores must complain with the characteristics defined by *FirmB*.

Recently, the distribution network has been complemented by owned stores, some of which directly managed by the firm. The main characteristics of these stores are large dimensions, prestigious locations in historic and commercial centres, and the fact that they carry all the products of *FirmB* brands.

The process

As explained by the chief information officer (CIO), given the variety in terms of products and geographical markets:

'Our capacity to keep pace derives from processes simplification and central-ised controls on all the delocalised and outsourced processes'.

Both upstream integration and partnership relationships with external sup-pliers make it possible for *FirmB* to exercise quality control over textiles and thread sooner. The materials are sent directly to the workshops and external producers without further controls, greatly reducing transport costs and lead times.

The production organisation maintains its strategic activities in the head-quarters' country based mainly on market sensitive issues, as faster response, time to market; and abroad, where efficiency is combined with the neces-sary cost control. The production model is arranged into a dual production line or supply chain, from which, 40% – including activities such as design, planning, coordination and programming – is carried out in the headquar-ters' country and 60% – including more operating activities – is delocalised, with a highly competitive network of suppliers.

FirmB manages also some total outsourced production, reserved for particu-lar products and specific markets like China. This area of activity has trig-gered competitive benefits within the organisation, in terms of cost reduction and shortening cycle times. In 2004, the Asian sourcing platform was com-pleted, which, with 40 specialists, ensures faster actions and better customer service in the Asian and the United States markets.

Regarding logistics and distribution, *FirmB* has decided to maintain direct control of it and has made investments on automating and integrating logis-tics processes. This model is supported by a centralised information tech-nology system, accessible from the various logistics centres. In this way, it is possible to coordinate, directly from the headquarters, the shipping of products according to required delivery date and geographic location of the customer, combining timeliness of information and better control of the business. *FirmB* has eliminated fragmentation of stocks across its interna-tional markets by directing the finished goods in three sorting centres, where a highly automated distribution system handles almost 50,000 packages a day.

The role of Information Technology

FirmB's network is based on total IT systems integration.

Concerning the foreign production centres, the IT manufacturing control system has enabled *FirmB* to closely monitor all the stages of manufacturing in different production units in real time and to make projection for the orders dispatch. This IT system has also been implemented for the logistics and distribution activities and also for managing the products sourced in the Far East.

A new project has recently been launched, involving a complete review of the processes, as production and logistics, and an updating of the IT system and procedures in use, in order to achieve a shorter time to market and with optimised customer deliveries.

Control and accounting issues: the findings

FirmB is one of the most complex organisations in the fashion industry. Many studies describe *FirmB* as unique for its structure: the more global it becomes, the more local it remains. Hence, it is worth asking which are the most important control and accounting issues faced by this complex but successful organisation.

In this section, contents and quotes from open-ended interviews undertaken with the controller and CIO of *FirmB* are reported, in order to present how the relationship among the different parties operating within the *FirmB* network are regulated. The purpose is to describe the role of management accounting and control mechanisms in such a complex network.

To give a thorough view of the findings, some important strings of the interview will be reported and commented by taking as a reference some of the concepts illustrated in the previous chapters, i.e. the governance and control structure (Chapters 3 and 4), performance, costing and collaborative programming issues (Chapter 5).

The governance and control structure

The governance model of *FirmB* is the one of a hierarchical type of network, characterised by different forms of controls, going from the input and process controls carried on through contractual specifications for the commercial partners, to the tight processes controls on the most strategic suppliers.

Regarding the characteristics of the inter-organisational relationships enter-tained by *FirmB*, the controller commented:

'We distinguish the supply network, upstream, the production network, and the distribution one downstream, or the *FirmB* agents around the world. [*Referring to the characteristics of the different inter-organisational relationships*] For example, with agents, the relationship is based on a formal contract. It may be short- or long-term oriented. With suppliers, the relationship is a bit closer, particularly with strategic suppliers. On the manufacturing side, almost all pro-duction poles are directly controlled by *FirmB*, this is due to the relevance of such locations hence the need to control them [...] despite the huge product range and the geographic dispersion, we want to maintain control through cen-tralised and highly simplified procedures and processes. For example, most of the manufacturing processes, even located abroad, are centrally coordinated'.

Performance measurement

On a monthly basis, *FirmB* assesses the performance of its external suppli-ers based on variance analysis. In fact, suppliers are paid each month, so such evaluation is necessary to invoice the right amounts, i.e. the amounts adjusted for any variance whose responsibility is on the partner. In any case, as stated by the CIO:

'The need to revise the actual amount of invoices is very rare. It is more fre-quent with the non-owned raw material suppliers rather than with our manu-facturing partners. Our outsourced manufacturing phases are quite simple. So once we have selected our external partners it is very unlikely that we have troubles with them'.

Regarding responsibilities on manufacturing variances, when asked about spoilages, the controller commented:

'If the inefficiency is on his [*the supplier*] side, then the supplier is responsible. If the spoilage is due to a material defect, then no responsibility is on the supplier'.

In any case, whenever there is an unexpected variance compared to perform-ance targets, as maintained by the CIO, *FirmB* tries to re-enact what hap-pened to understand who is accountable. There is not a 'unilateral' view in this respect. *FirmB* tends to adopt a balanced view on problematic situations, thanks to consultation with the counterpart.

Quality standards of external suppliers are also assessed by *FirmB*:

'On the quality side, we ask basically technical information and we also carry out inspecting activities. There are many workshops for different phases of the manufacturing process; however I [*the controller*] have set an internal paper, a kind of sheet where all information is gathered, and is available to us, regarding each of our supplier partners. With such a tool I can even monitor the single order consumption rate till completion [...] Suppliers who do not meet time requirements are also obliged to pay a penalty to our firm'.

Inspecting activities are also important for evaluating the performance of supplier partners:

'We have an important technical office, called 'times and methods department', which assesses the performance trends with each supplier. The output of such studies is the definition of cost rates per hour, concerning the manufacturing of an item or phase from a certain supplier. So, it is possible to evaluate its performance based on average rates of past collaboration, in terms of cost, times, quality, defect rates, etc.'

The controller specified that *FirmB* elaborates, for each external partner, an income statement for internal uses only. In this elaboration, suppliers are not involved nor they get such information from *FirmB*. The collaboration of suppliers, in this respect, is related to the provision of information on manufacturing cost items. The other income statement elements are estimated by *FirmB* on the basis of past experience:

'We have the knowledge of the process as well as a long history in this business on the basis of which we are able to provide an income statement for each of our external manufacturers'.

The same logic is applied for assessing the performance of stores. *FirmB* is able to define an income statement for each of its stores, both owned and franchised:

'What they buy from us and the selling price (hence the margin we grant them) are something we know. We need to have from them the detail of their costs, among which the rent is usually the highest one, and the percentage of sale goods on total revenues'.

Collaborative planning
Regarding programming, the collaborative logic underlying such activity is to be found in the fact that although production needs can vary a lot during the year, *FirmB* always wants to saturate the production capacity of its

external manufacturers along the whole year. On this point, the controller commented:

'If they need to invest in equipment, it is fundamental that we grant them a certain stability of turnover. Therefore, we basically define some specific mixes of products for each of our suppliers so that they are busy all the year'.

Costing issues

Within the production department of *FirmB*, there is a team of people – technical staff – in charge of defining the target costs of more than 6,000 products. The items of the unitary product costs in *FirmB* are defined as being the following:

- Direct materials;
- Transformation costs.

As explained by the controller, *FirmB* technical staff defines a standard cost whose amount is the basis for negotiating the acquisition price with suppliers, according to a cost-plus method. Given the experience of the firm and the stability of relationships with external manufacturers, the variances are at maximum 1% of total production costs.

Costing issues are fundamental within the initial negotiation process with external manufacturers. Such negotiation also represents one of the most important moments impacting on the development and stability of the relationship. Referring to the price *FirmB* proposes to suppliers, the controller specified:

'We use a cost-plus system. This, however, is not a pure system, because after the price is determined, there are some analyses finalised to understand if that price is feasible in that specific market. If the price is not appropriate, there is an inverse process aiming at determining some cost reductions, or profit margins reductions. This reminds a kind of target costing process'.

Cost and other management accounting information exchanges

From the interview analysis, it emerges that *FirmB* has built its network, and continues to enlarge it, through exerting control by requiring quite intensive information exchanges from its partners. Information exchange issues are fundamental in the management of *FirmB* interorganisational relationships, with a special emphasis on those exchanges taking place during the earliest stages of the relationship development. On this topic, the controller explained that:

'Information exchanges are usually intense at the beginning of the relationships, while setting up terms and conditions. The most important information in this phase are, of course, related to cycle time, delivery time, costs, and the price. Afterwards, when manufacturing activities are carried out by our partners, there are other information exchanges, more related to technical matters. We are not much advanced on this side, due to our previous vertical integration'.

Concerning, more specifically, accounting information exchanges, these are fundamental in the governance model adopted by *FirmB* for the control of both the manufacturing network and the distribution one, as stated by the controller:

'On the financial side, I know almost everything about the supplier. I have the knowledge and the story to perform a sort of profit and loss statement of every important supplier, typically the small sized ones, with a limited production capacity, and a long-term relation with us. These are closer suppliers. On the retail side, we have some key information on the franchisees: the purchased quantities, the price to the final customer, the main expenses of the store, as the rental fee, and the sales trend, that is how much the store sells during each collection and how much in the "sold" phase'.

When explicitly asked to explain the role of management accounting in controlling the relationships with external parties, the controller added:

'Management accounting is fundamental. With numbers we manage centrally all subsidiaries, the manufacturing poles with their local networks and the distribution side, agents and retailers. The management accounting view is on the whole network, on its overall performance. Information is collected directly from each subsidiary, or indirectly, through different channels. The fundamental role of management accounting is the pricing of every item of the collections. The pricing process is of course based on detailed analysis of profit margins.

There are two essential moments related to the use of management accounting: the budgeting process and the pricing process. The two are related in some way, because if there are inaccuracies in the pricing process, then the actual analysis will show them. Another important role for management accounting is the assessment of stores that *FirmB* owns and manages directly. There are capital expenditures on such stores and a good evaluation helps identifying critical success factors [...] We need to perform cost–benefit analysis to understand whether it is better to buy a store and give it to some external partner to manage it or to manage it directly. [...] Given that there is not a supply chain manager it is the controller the key actor in this processes. He is not only the man of numbers, but also the one in charge of managing the timing of all our dispersed activities. He is the coordinator'.

Table 6.6 summarises the characteristics of the external relationships of *FirmB* with its different counterparts and reports the specifics of management control patterns and accounting information exchanges.

Evidence from *FirmC*

Company overview

FirmC operates in the sports and leisure apparel, footwear and accessories industry through different brands. The firm is managed by a headquarter, which carries out service activities, such as product research and development, marketing and communication, and information technology management.

FirmC bases its activities primarily on business relationships with independent firms, which receive *FirmC's* trademarks through licensing agreements. Currently, the network is made up of 50 licensees, which cover more than 90 markets worldwide.

In addition, *FirmC* has outsourced its manufacturing processes to third parties, and supervises and optimises, via specific sourcing centres, all manufacturing phases on behalf of licensees. The firm monitors and assesses the quality of the products distributed by these independent business partners, focusing attention to the supply of finished goods from production sources to different target markets. Normally *FirmC* buys finished products after providing technical specifications on the characteristics of the raw materials and the manufacturing process. The growth strategies and the marketing tools are centrally coordinated. *FirmC* aims at becoming a worldwide leader in the casual and sports apparel industry. The total revenues of *FirmC* in 2004 were around 100,000 million euro with an operating income of 6 million euro and an ROI of approximately 6%.

The business model

FirmC's business system is developed around a network model. The company identifies in the licensee a business partner for the diffusion and distribution of its products throughout the world. The company's goal is to propose partners a range of integrated services, not simply a product. This innovative,

Table 6.6 Findings on *FirmB*.

Variables and issues	Partners			
	Textile and yarn suppliers	Foreign manufacturing subsidiaries	Small and mid-size subcontractors	Commercial network
Description of the counterparts	Third parties partially owned by *FirmB*	Foreign subsidiaries, totally or partially owned and directly managed by *FirmB*. These are foreign manufacturing poles managing outsourced production in their region	Local, independent third parties in charge of labour intensive production phases	Mainly stores with franchising agreements and some owned stores
Relationship life cycle	Integration is quite recent but relationships are long term	Even the most recent subsidiaries are managed by ex-*FirmB* managers having a long relationship with the firm	Long, mature relationships	Long-term relationships
Reasons for collaboration	Time compression	To be more competitive locally thanks to the possibility of controlling, through the subsidiaries, a network of local suppliers	Flexibility and efficiency (labour cost differentials)	Reputation and knowledge of customers' behaviour (for owned stores) Leverage on local entrepreneurship to enhance profitability and responsiveness (for franchisees)
Governance structure	Hierarchical relationships (based on equity ownership)	Hierarchical relationships (based on equity ownership)	Hierarchical-based to trust-based pattern	Hierarchical relationships (for owned stores) Hierarchical-like, contractual relationships (for franchising stores)

Interdependencies	Sequential interdependence for operations	Reciprocal interdependence for operations at the single relationship level	High sequential interdependence	Sequential interdependence
Knowledge on the transformation process	High due to vertical integration	High (the business model of subsidiaries is the one of *FirmB*)	High	High
Output measurability	High output measurability both in financial and non-financial terms	High output measurability both in financial and non-financial terms	High output measurability both in financial and non-financial terms	High output measurability both in financial and non-financial terms
Forms of control	Control is based on equity ownership and inputs control (inspection activities, quality controls)	*FirmB* chooses what should be produced by each of the foreign manufacturers, which then independently decide how to allocate the production tasks among their network of small medium enterprises. The controls are focused most on outputs and process cost control and efficiency	Control is focused on output and on processes (through inspection activities). There are both ex ante (budgets) and ex post mechanisms (variance analysis and other non-financial performance indicators)	Output control based on ex post mechanisms is possible both for owned and franchisees. *FirmB* can evaluate performance through a P&L for each store

(continued)

Table 6.6 (continued).

Variables and issues		Partners		
	Textile and yarn suppliers	Foreign manufacturing subsidiaries	Small and mid-size subcontractors	Commercial network
Performance measurement	Quality and timeliness indicators	Mainly productivity indicators, waste/efficiency indicators	At the beginning of the relationship, detailed information on cycle time, delivery time, costs, and the price. Quality indicators, productivity indicators, waste/efficiency indicators in later stages of the relationship and a P&L for the most strategic suppliers	Purchased quantities, prices, the main expenses of the store (e.g. rent), how much the store sells during each collection and how much in the 'sold' phase
Inter-organisational cost management practices (IOCM)	Not relevant	Cost-plus system for defining transfer prices	There is a kind of cost-plus system, supported by target costing	Not relevant

Cost and management accounting information exchanges	Information exchanges are mainly based on price, lead times and delivery times	Due to direct control of the subsidiaries, information exchanges are both financial and non-financial	Information exchanges are both financial and non financial (prices, profit margins, target costs, quantities, cycle times, lead times, spoilage, and defect rates)	Information exchanges are on financial data and expenses of the store/distributor, on sales quantity and sales mixes
Inter-firm information systems	Under development	An inter-firm information system enabling *FirmB* to monitor manufacturing stages in different production units in real time and to make projection for order dispatches	An inter-firm information system supporting regular information flows between parties	All the stores are connected with *FirmB* through an integrated information system
The role of management accounting (MA)	MA has an important role in negotiating and setting conditions and terms of the relationship (mainly transfer prices)	MA plays a fundamental role both as an ex ante (budgeting) and as an ex post control (performance evaluation)	MA plays a fundamental role both as an ex ante (budgeting) and as an ex post control (performance evaluation)	MA has an important role in the performance assessment of both the franchisees and the owned stores

flexible and modular business system allows the company to grow rapidly, both in-house or internally (through new licensees and collaborating enterprises) and externally (through new trademarks and business lines), while maintaining a lean and agile structure. This large network is made up of independent small companies, linked by means of a new technology, in a data processing platform completely integrated to the network through internet. Web integration is studied to share, exchange and exploit information in real time.

The actors of the network

The network is made up of different entities:

- *FirmC*;
- Licensees;
- Sourcing centres;
- Trading companies;
- External factories.

FirmC carries out various activities, going from the development and coordination of the entire network, the trademark and product positioning, the communication and global marketing strategy to product concept and industrialisation: creative thinking, product research and development, product procurement through sourcing centres; operational management. It is responsible for the success of the business and the economic and financial sustainability of the entire network.

The licensees, settled on a geographical basis, are responsible for supplying the products to retailers, as well as for local marketing policies, following the *FirmC*'s guidelines. They use area managers for coordinating the relationships with retailers in specific geographical domains.

The sourcing centres are companies in charge of providing products to licensees and of all the activities related to their logistic issues.

'The sourcing centres negotiate with factories for the best price possible. The sourcing centres, in turn, [...] have to price a product in order to gain commission rates from licensees. Obviously, sourcing centres are paying special attention to alternative factories, searching better prices or improving effectiveness. However, it is quite easy to switch from one factory to another, without much trouble'*(The Controller)*.

The trading companies operate as a purchase or a manufacturing department. They produce the samples, according to the specifications provided, and sell them to *FirmC*. They also collect all the orders of the various products and interact with the factories to produce them.

> '*Trading companies* are joint ventures owned by *FirmC* at 50%. The other partner, the remaining 50%, is the main trader in Hong Kong. This joint venture operates as a purchasing office, or as a manufacturer' *(The Controller)*.

The factories are third parties involved in the manufacturing of the products according to both the requirements provided by *FirmC* and the volumes required by the sourcing centres. Once completed the manufacturing process, they send the products directly to retailers.

> 'The factories quote for us a final price, on the finished product [...] but we are not involved in the buying of raw materials so upstream'*(The Controller)*.

The structure of *FirmC*

FirmC is organised around different departments that are responsible for various activities:

(1) *The Bidding Department* is in charge of managing the negotiation phase with third parties that manufacture items for the licensees. This phase involves the trading companies and the sourcing centres.

(2) *The Country Department* is responsible for representing the whole set of licensees network with which *FirmC* collaborates. The licensees do not purchase products/items directly from *FirmC*, but from the factories, and pay a fee to the trading companies.

(3) *The Factory Department* is in charge of managing the manufacturing activities. Licensees submit orders to the sourcing centres on items of the collection, via web. External factories take care of the manufacturing process, primarily in Asia, through continuous contacts with local partners.

(4) *The Forecast Department* manages the interaction with the licensees and makes predictions on sales and production quantities.

(5) *The Marketing Department* is responsible for setting global marketing policies and supervising licensees.

(6) *The Samples Department* designs collections, one of the major sources of profit for *FirmC*.

(7) *The Specs Department* is responsible for determining the technical specificities of every item and transmits it to the trading companies and to the sourcing centres. The department intervene in two

moments. First, in the collection phase, with the 'tailor men', who provides them a detailed product configuration. Second, it gets involved before the beginning of the manufacturing process, with an intense communication between *FirmC*, the trading companies and the sourcing centres on more detailed technical information. The goal is to obtain identical products from different factories.

The retail strategy

Throughout 2004, *FirmC* developed a retail project aimed at reaching directly the end-customer through a broad and structured presence, embedded in the firm business system. The project includes four 'Concept Stores' directly owned by *FirmC* or in franchising:

(1) The single-brand store, used for a classic/sports range of stylish apparel.
(2) The small single-trademark stores, used for designed footwear collections and accessories.
(3) The 'brand outlet', used for a portfolio of *FirmC*'s trademarks.
(4) The big size store offering a multi-branched array of stock at attractive prices.

The adoption of this new retail strategy aims to have a direct contact with the customers to understand their specific needs. To this end, *FirmC* has decided to develop this strategy in Italy and use the information collected from the customers to provide guidelines and suggestions related to product characteristics to other countries.

Control and accounting issues: the findings on FirmC

In this section, contents and quotes from open-ended interviews undertaken with the controller of *FirmC* are reported, in order to present how the relationship among the different parties operating within the *FirmC* network – the licensees, the sourcing centres, the trading companies, the external factories – are regulated. The purpose is to describe the role of management accounting and control mechanisms in such a complex network.

FirmC is a typical network of interorganisational relationships managed all over the world. Its hybrid connections range from licensing agreements for manufacturing and for distributing, to joint ventures, and franchising agreements.

To give a thorough view of the findings, some important strings of the interview will be reported and commented by taking as a reference some of the concepts illustrated in the previous chapters, i.e. the governance and control structure (Chapters 3 and 4), performance, costing and collaborative programming issues (Chapter 5).

The governance and control structure

The relationships between the different entities of the network tend to be market based. In fact, the transactions carried out are regulated mainly by means of a formal contract. It is in this contract that all the terms and conditions of the activities that each party has to carry out are specified. For example with reference to licensees and their level of autonomy the controller said:

> 'They are entrepreneurs, completely autonomous, which work independently. For the development of their business they have some contractual constraints related to product positioning – deriving from the characteristics of the products and the price ranges – to geographical competence [...] [they] must comply with general conditions, but can operate as they want [...]'.

The relationships between the entities tend to be regulated by means of information technology and the data processing platform, which are the key strategic *specific asset* of the firm. The platform has been conceived and developed by means of a full integration via web, which is seen as an effective means for communication between the entities of the network. Web integration is required to link single partners to *FirmC*, to connect the partners and introduce communication among them.

> 'Our web integrated information system is one of the most important assets; it permits to exchange information all over the network [...]. It connects everyone to everyone else'*(The Controller).*

The information exchanged in the network is mainly technical and functional to the operating activities aimed at producing, distributing and selling the products.

> 'Orders are centrally managed and consolidated. The required quantity, based on the consolidated orders, is sent to the chosen factories for manufacturing. The factories, then, send the finished goods to the licensees, based on single orders' *(The Controller).*

On the economic side, transactions are regulated by defining a specific price. As the controller suggested:

> 'The main objective is to have a product that has a price structure that is, on average, applicable by all licensees [...] and considering that [...] given a wholesale price as a result of purchase cost plus margin, the local distributor, to survive, takes this purchase price FOB and adds customs and tariffs and adds his own margin to have enough resources to invest in advertising and generate profit ... we collect the final price at which our items are sold on the different markets. We do this for certain categories but when we have 1,000 items it does not make sense [...] Having information on the specific prices applied in the different markets is not really useful for us'.

The collaborative planning

The plan of the activities that *FirmC* has to carry out when collaborating with the other actors of the network follows specific steps and is particularly articulated and detailed. The *Samples Department* develops the samples offering several 'business opportunities' to the licensees. The licensees select and purchase the samples they think are suitable for their sales campaign. The samples are produced by means of the trading companies and then delivered. At the same time, the *Forecast Department* starts forecasting sales and production, communicating directly with the licensees that have purchased the samples. On the basis of the products actually purchased by the licensees and the volume of the forecasts, the *Specs Department* completes the technical specifications necessary for the production phase. The technical specifications and the quantities are fundamental elements that enable a third division of *FirmC*, the *Biddings Department*, to assign the production to the trading companies. The licensees are then ready to place their orders through the *Factory Department*, which collectively manages the production progress, quality control, and administrative issues together with the trading companies.

The plan is prepared by means of e-processes. By means of online transactions, the various actors of the network propose specific requirements to other divisions so that they can be discussed, negotiated and approved in a short period of time.

Performance measurement

Given the business model, *FirmC* measures financial performance in a very simple way. They prepare an income statement with a very simple structure. Revenues are related to royalties from sales of licensees and from samples sales. These revenues are traceable to specific licensees and brands.

With reference to costs, the only costs that can be directly assigned to the brand is the cost of samples. After that all the other costs are not distinguished by brand. The only other cost that could be split over the brands is the cost of communication, but this is not always the case because the communication campaigns are not all the time referred to one brand but to families of brands.

'I just know the royalties that any licensee pays, and that's it! I know the sales of every licensee. I precisely know what any licensee does, because they have to get authorisation from the headquarter for all these operations: items and quantities. But a detailed analysis for single brand is not necessary for us. We just manage and develop such brands and get royalties. That's our business' *(The Controller).*

'*[Brand]* costs are related to the development of the sample collection for every brand; at this level the costs are known. But any further subdivision for the moment seems nonsense, due to a lack of real direct costs. Of course, I should find appropriate drivers, but it is a quite not-precise exercise, so we remain at this level of detail' *(The Controller).*

While the analysis is conducted with reference to costs of developing a sample, the collection of cost information on the manufacturing process depends on the level of maturity of the product and its level of complexity. The more mature is the product and the lower the level of complexity, the lower the need to collect specific cost information to make production and price decisions.

'[...] I do not care how much it costs to produce a T-Shirt [...]. On the contrary, if I launch a new product or shoe I do care because there are shoes that have 10–12 layers for a sole [...] every sole is made in a different way [...] each size has a different die, so according to the design the cost changes enormously [...] there I want to know the cost. But for a T-shirt I do not need that information because it is an extremely mature product [...] For a wind coat it is necessary, it must be on the market. I cannot offer a coat at a cost of 1500 euros because I do not sell it. But I can decide to produce a jacket whose cost is 500 euros that is as more technical as possible [...] so that I invest in lower margins because I want to make that jacket as a leading product of my collection, there I need to know the cost'*(The Controller).*

Cost and other management accounting information exchanges
As regards the exchange of information between the actors of the network, the controller suggested the following:

'The kind of information ranges from price, quantities, costs, everything concerning accounting, to the patterns for the factories or production units' *(The Controller).*

More specifically, with reference to the different partners, the controller indicated:

'Information is exchanged between the licensees and the area managers, which share that information inside the network. Information is about *prices, costs, promotions, national markets*. So, *FirmC* has a thorough view on each market and on each player. This is very useful, because we try to have similar market positions and pricing policies globally, even if the price, per se, is not the same in all markets'.

'According to the *technical information* provided by *FirmC*, this company [*the trading company*] manufactures the sample collections, or part of it, and sends it back to *FirmC*, that is supposed to sell them'.

'*Factories* point on efficiency rates and on scale economies'. 'Usually we indicate how should be the fabrics, we suggest some *technical features*, some *quality standards*'.

'The information shared between the sourcing centres and *FirmC* is simply price, the final price of a given item'.

Table 6.7 summarises the characteristics of the relationships that *FirmC* has with its external partners and reports the specifics of management control patterns and accounting information exchanges.

Evidence from *FirmD*

Company overview

FirmD is a fashion company dedicated to the design, production and distribution of luxury goods. The company produces and distributes a high range of products. It operates in different market segments related to clothing, knitwear, lingerie and swimwear, leather goods, handbags, shoes, various accessories, eyewear and perfumes. It owns various trademarks. Over time it has acquired equity stake in other companies. In addition, it has undertaken license agreements with well-known fashion designers. Products are realised and sold under license agreements with independent manufacturers and third-party distributors. The company owns a few stores, after a process of integration downstream the supply chain, and manages also some sales branches in the main European countries and in the USA.

Most of the processes such as presentation of collections and production, sales and distribution are managed directly by *FirmD*, whereas the definition of style and the communication campaigns are carried out with the collaboration of fashion houses.

Table 6.7 Findings on *FirmC*.

Variables and issues	Partners				
	Licensees	Sourcing centres	Trading companies	External factories
Description of the counterparts	Interfirm relationships based on licensing agreements for the distribution of *FirmC* products	Partner firms, that act as intermediaries between *FirmC* and the licensees	Joint ventures that interact with local factories in Asia for the production and with the licensees for distribution	Independent third parties or outsourcees. They interface with the sourcing centres to sell the finished products
Relationship life cycle	Consolidated long term relationships	Consolidated long term relationships	Consolidated long term relationships based on equity ownership (joint venture)	Temporary. It is often quite easy to switch from one factory to the other
Reasons for collaboration	Reciprocity: *FirmC* represents an ideal partner for the development of the product, whereas licensees are complementary partners in the sales activity	Flexibility in the selection and relationships with the factories	Flexibility in combining sample design and manufacturing requirements	Efficiency in the manufacturing process
Governance structure	Market based (hierarchy based only with reference to some constraints related to product positioning, geographical competence, and so on).	Market based to hierarchy based	Market based	Market based: they are second-tier relationships

(continued)

Table 6.7 (continued).

Variables and issues	Partners			
	Licensees	Sourcing centres	Trading companies	External factories
Interdependencies	Interdependencies exist, but *FirmC* has greater bargaining power. It needs the licensees to reach markets all over the world. For the licensees *FirmC* is a fundamental business partner	Reciprocal to pooled interdependencies: sourcing centres and *FirmC* have almost the same interests	Reciprocal to pooled interdependencies	No direct interdependences. They are mediated by sourcing centers and trading companies
Knowledge on the transformation process	*FirmC* has a thorough knowledge of the licensees, but the commercial process is not always completely known because it varies according to the geographical areas	Sourcing centres are related to *FirmC*. Interactions are frequent and reciprocal knowledge is high	There is reciprocal knowledge only for some parts of the process (on the commercial side the knowledge is more limited)	*FirmC* provides factories with detailed technical specifications, which they should follow strictly
Output measurability	Relatively high output measurability based on financial information	High output measurability based on both financial and non-financial information	Medium to high output measurability	High output measurability related to the number of units produced

Forms of control	Control is mostly based on output control, based on ex ante mechanisms (articulated planning process) and ex post mechanism (measurement of national market shares, customer satisfaction and so on)	Control is possible both through process control and through output control, based on ex ante and ex post mechanisms. Sourcing centres are responsible for efficiency and effectiveness improvement, choosing the best factories and supplying the product to licensees	Control is based on contractual agreements, basically on price mechanisms. There is however, the possibility to control the output of the relationship: efficiency and effectiveness of the production process	Control is based on contract clauses
Performance measurement	FirmC evaluates licensees' performance based on market indicators (licensees pay royalties and fees based on sales)	Financial results assessment, efficiency indicators, quality indicators, etc.	Market indicators, time indicators, quality indicators, etc.	There are some productivity indicators (costs, efficiency, etc.) quality indicators, cycle time indicators, delivery time indicators
Inter-organisational cost management practices (IOCM)	None	More intense share of cost information, but no IOCM practices	None	None

(continued)

Table 6.7 (continued).

Variables and issues	Partners			
	Licensees	Sourcing centres	Trading companies	External factories
Cost and management accounting information exchanges	Exchange of information concerning the prices applied, promotion costs, national markets indicators	Financial information exchanged are mainly related to prices, while non financial information exchanged refer to the entire manufacturing process	Exchange of information concerning the sample manufacturing process	The information exchanged mainly refer to efficiency rates, scale economies, technical features, quality standards
Inter-firm information systems	A web integrated interfirm information system exists. It links all actors to each other in real time	A web integrated interfirm information system exists. It links all actors to each other in real time	A web integrated interfirm information system exists. It links all actors to each other in real time	A web integrated interfirm information system exists. It links all actors to each other in real time
The role of management accounting (MA)	MA contributes in the negotiation phase and in performance evaluation	MA role is to support planning and controlling sourcing centres' operations	MA supports the plans and the measurement of production and market results	No specific role

FirmD has about 120 exclusive points of sale as mono-brand shops and shops-in-shop, and over 2,500 points of sale including multi-brand boutiques, corners, and department stores. In the distribution process *FirmD* is involved in three main areas of activities: managing showrooms; managing showrooms held by agents and/or importers bounded to *FirmD* by exclusive contracts; exclusive direct or franchised sales points.

The total revenues of *FirmD* in 2004 were around 250 million euro with an operating income of 22 million euro and an ROI of approximately 9%.

The business model

The actors of the network

FirmD operates through a network of firms that are responsible for carrying out various activities at different stages of the value chain. The entities involved are the following:

- *FirmD*;
- Raw materials suppliers;
- Façonists;
- Finished product suppliers;
- Agents.

FirmD takes care of manufacturing samples, presentation of collections, sales management, and the purchasing process. Other activities carried out by the firm are the planning process and the coordination of external suppliers and manufacturers. The company is also involved in the distribution and the post-sale activities.

Raw materials suppliers provide *FirmD* with fabric, wool, thread, buttons and other accessories necessary to manufacture the products.

When collections are characterised by high content of style and design, thus requiring continuous innovation through materials, the suppliers are selected *ad hoc* to comply with the specific requirements of the products. On the contrary, for continually produced fabrics, the group of suppliers is more stable and the relationships developed with them are closer. In 2004, there were approximately 65 suppliers of fabrics and accessories on each collection, ten of which were mainly located in India, China and Turkey.

Façonists are small-sized external laboratories (over 95% of them operate with less than ten employees) and are specialised in a specific work activity:

cutting, making-up and ironing, together with other activities such as embroidery, printing, etc.

> 'The *façonist* does not participate in the development process, except for the final phase of sample production and the series that are sent to the agents [...] All the development is done internally or, if it is delegated, only part of it is assigned to the *façonist* [...] the design *strictu sensu*, including the development of the paper model, the test of the paper model, the study of the different working problems etc., is carried out internally, and the *façonist* intervenes only in some phases of the manufacturing process [...] *(Technical Director for Foreign Activities)*.

Only a few of them are located outside the country, in Eastern Europe, due to the low cost of labour. The geographical proximity of most of these workshops is an aspect that the company considers of strategic relevance, because a lower distance allows a tighter control over the manufacturing processes, in terms of quality standards and cycle/delivery times.

Finished products suppliers are in charge of producing completed goods, carrying out activities from the development of the paper model, the selection of the suppliers, the purchase of raw materials, to the manufacturing of products and the final delivery to *FirmD*.

> 'The supplier of finished products receives from us a certain number of data and develops directly the paper model, solves those problems that are related to the manufacturing of a cloth, produces the prototype that is valid for trials, which will be tested here in the firm, and after a certain number of corrections and trials, it is refined and made available for sale'*(Technical Director for Foreign Activities)*.

Agents are responsible for the sales of *FirmD*'s products both in national and foreign markets. Currently, there are 30 agents responsible for domestic sales and 6–8 agents responsible for international sales. They are organisations with which *FirmD* has consolidated relationships, as suggested by the commercial director for Italy:

> 'They work with us from the very beginning, they have been working for us for at least 10–12 years. Therefore, we can say that we have a very consolidated structure that gives us the opportunity to have reliant relationships'.

Control and accounting issues: the findings on FirmD

To give a thorough view of the findings, in this section some important strings of the interview will be reported and commented by taking as a reference some of the concepts illustrated in the previous chapters, i.e. the governance and control structure (Chapters 3 and 4), performance, costing and collaborative programming issues (Chapter 5).

The governance and control structure

As emerging from the overview, the firm acts in a highly complex network of interfirm relations. These latter are of different nature and range from market based, to very bureaucratic and centralised ones, and there is also a considerable group of mixed relationships. This difference is particularly clear with reference to the distinction between *façonists* and finished product suppliers. The first are in charge of executing specific phases of the manufacturing process. In this case, *FirmD* provides them with the raw materials or work in progress which needs to be worked. The second concern external manufacturers or laboratories which provide *FirmD* with finished goods on the basis of the specifications indicated. Suppliers are involved from the very beginning of product development and receive from *FirmD* very detailed information and specifications on the product characteristics and features.

> '*FirmD* usually provides the *façonists* with the paper-based pattern and a *technical sheet*, containing all types of information required to realise the prototype. The technical sheet is a kind of document, a very detailed one, which explains to the manufacturer all issues about the prototype, like size-measures, raw materials, accessories. The *façonist* provides us finished goods following our specifications.

> The suppliers, on the contrary, not only intervene in internal processes, they are part of the development process. *FirmD* provides the supplier with all necessary information, and this one develops the pattern, and concludes the process with a prototype. After this, *FirmD* and specialists inside the company controls this output. Then an interactive process of corrections takes place, until the sample is perfect.

> So, relationships are very different. A *façonist* producer execute only what is determined or specified ex-ante, in certain production phases; the supplier is of course a closer partner' *(Technical Director for Italian Activities).*

The collaborative planning

Once the sales campaign is terminated, one of the most critical activities is related to planning the manufacturing process. This is particularly complex and articulated in *FirmD* because this latter puts a great effort in ensuring that the capacity of all the different collaborating laboratories is properly filled in, starting from those laboratories that are more critical for the production of *FirmD's* products.

157

'At the end of the sales campaign, there is a huge number of things to produce. So Davidson (pseudonym) says 'In order to fill my laboratories in Hungary, as last year we had a small loss, I need 95,000 pieces of apparel'; Cox (pseudonym) says that for his Italian laboratories he needs a certain number of pieces to produce, because they are the wealth of the company and they must therefore survive. I say then that given 100%, only 28–29% of units sold go to Hungary, while the remaining stays in Italy. We organise to maintain a profit that is worth this name, because otherwise we cannot justify our presence within the company. After that, all the technical issues arise, we carry out all our controls and then we proceed'(Technical Director for Italian Activities).

In addition the planning should be managed carefully and is a critical activity in the case of *façonists*. This is because each *façonist* is in charge of the execution of a specific phase of the process. Therefore, *FirmD* needs to program in great detail who has to do what, by which deadline and within which budget. It is this ex-ante control mechanism that guarantees a full coordination of high number of entities involved in the same manufacturing process.

Performance measurement

In *FirmD*, the examination of actual performance is undertaken by using different income statements referred to various dimensions, and a variance analysis. The dimensions that are actually monitored are the single line, the brand, and the type of product (Figures 6.13 and 6.14).

'We prepare an income statement for each line. Obviously each brand includes more lines. We have different parameters of cost accounting and with reference to each of these parameters we go from the brand to the single line. Let me just explain a bit better. The brand 'X' includes 'X collection' and 'X precollection', for example. A subbrand is 'Y' which is also, in turn, split in three collections; then we go in further more detail because we decompose the collection in apparel and accessories. Thus, we prepare an income statement 'Y apparel collection' and 'Y accessories collection'(The Controller).

In addition, one of the specifics of *FirmD*, which is rarely seen in firms operating in other industries, but also in firms belonging to the fashion sector, is the income statement of the collection.

'When we prepare our line income statements we always refer to seasons, and as you may understand, the sum of the two seasons is never a year because two seasons overlap […] Now we have a forecast before summer 2005 and a forecast fall/winter 2005. For the spring/summer 2005 we have a global report and then a report for each apparel line, a report for the accessories line; thus we have the

	Actual		Budget	
	No. of pieces	Average price	No. of pieces	Average price
Description	Value	% on net sales	Value	% on net sales
Sales Italy				
Sales abroad				
Exchange rate variance				
Sales retail				
Royalties				
Sales from inventory available				
Other sales				
Gross sales				
Returns				
Discounts				
Cancellations				
Net sales				
Purchase of raw materials				
Ending inventory of raw materials at market price				
Raw materials usage				
Purchase of finished products				
External work				
Ending inventory of finished products at market price				
Cost of goods sold				
INDUSTRIAL GROSS PROFIT				
Collection unit				
Models unit				
Prototypes unit				
Total R&D costs				
Raw materials and finished products sample (net of use of raw materials in production)				
External work for sample				
Direct sample costs				
Total sample costs				
Royalties				
Commissions				
Line advertisement				
Fairs and exhibitions				
Transport cost for sales				
Other direct commercial costs				
Direct commercial costs				
Boutique				
Showroom				
Direct commercial personnel costs				

Figure 6.13 Line income statement

brand 'Y' and we start with the pre-collection line 'Y', we have a main 'Y' line with its income statement, then we have 'X', 'Z' and then the pre-collection accessories line 'Y' [...] in other words this is the logic for all the brands of the group' (*The Controller*).

159

Size development centre Technical unit Time and methods unit Raw materials purchases unit Fabric control unit Transports Fabric inventory Knitting inventory Preparation for external work Haberdashery inventory Cutting department Programming department Embroidery special work abroad Embroidery special work Italy Work in progress management Italy Work in progress management, knitting Work in progress at home Test – receiving Test – knitting Foreign manufacturing **Cost of production personnel related to the line** **LINE SEGMENT MARGIN** Board of directors and managing direction Technical – manufacturing direction Management accounting Personnel department Information systems department Retail management Facilities management Marketing Financial accounting Treasury General affairs Milan Reception General/maintenance services **Cost of general and administrative personnel** Other manufacturing costs (manufacturing depreciation) Other commercial costs (depreciation goods at third parties' place, cost of boutiques) Other general costs (general depreciation, commercial expenses, bank expenses) Headquarter fixed costs allocated **OPERATING INCOME**	

Figure 6.13   *(continued)*

Costing issues

The costing system is organised around cost centres and takes into consideration the reference to season when collecting and recording data. This is the basis for preparing the income statement for each collection.

Brand 'X'-Milan

	Actual	%	Budget	%
Sales				
Other revenues				
Production value				
Cost of goods sold				
Beginning inventory				
Purchases				
Other purchases				
Ending inventory				
Costs for commercial and administrative services				
Credit cards fee				
Commercial consulting				
Advertising and marketing costs				
Other commercial costs				
Board of directors compensation				
Accounting consulting				
Utilities				
Other general and administrative costs				
Costs of third parties assets usage				
Value added				
Personnel costs				
EBITDA				
Operating amortisation and depreciation				
Intangible assets				
Tangible assets				
Losses on accounts receivables/provisions/ impairment				
Other operating costs				
EBIT				
Gains from participation				
Net financial income (charges)				
Total of non-operating revenues and costs				
Current income				
Amortisation of goodwill/brands				
Extraordinary income				
Extraordinary expenses				
Total of non-current revenues and costs				
Pre-tax income (loss)				
Taxes				
Net income (loss)				

Figure 6.14 Brand income statement

'Conventionally fixed costs are those in the accounting and finance departments and in all the other support units. Conventionally, they are split in
two, and the first six months are allocated to one collection and the second to
the other. The other costs are the cost of sample and of all the organisational
units that are related to sample [...]. The costs that we incur right now refer to
spring/summer 2005 season, so the revenues of this season will be considered

in the next year [...]. In this case the costs are postponed to the next year. This year the costs of the last year are considered, so we are not matched [...]. Now we are preparing the sample fall/winter 2005, then after March, spring/summer. So in the general ledger, costs are referred to the right season: they are the costs of sample, the direct costs (raw materials and production) and all the personnel costs, which are particularly relevant for us, related to units of models, proto-types and collection' (*The Controller*).

Cost and other management accounting information exchanges

What emerges from the analysis of the case is that the higher the level of information exchanges, the better the control is over collaborating partners. With reference to *façonists* there are specific mechanisms that are used both in the sample production phase and the work and rework step:

'In the samples production phase there is not much time to control the produc-ers on spoilages, etc. Of course, in the manufacturing phase these analyses are a routine. For what concerns variances, there is a threshold for spoilages, rework, and the materials consumption. If the threshold is exceeded, there starts an examination process, aimed at understanding the causes that originate such changes. This process consists in comparing the average consumption rate of different periods. If there are reasonable causes behind this, none is blamed, so the *façonist* or the workshop is not responsible at all.

On the work and rework side, issues are more complex. There is a specific study office that, in the samples phase, gathers information on every item, regarding the kind of treatment of work related to the time needed to perform it. They deter-mine a '*cost per minute*', it's a kind of coefficient, related to the complexity of every collection/item, to the area where production takes place, etc. Anyway, we have continuous relationships with our partners; we know the way they work'.

See Figure 6.15 for a summary report of variances.

The investigation of variances is particularly critical with reference to raw materials, because their use is difficult to predetermine in detail.

'Things are a bit more complex in the case of use of raw materials. Consider that 25–30% of fabric is managed within the firm. I want to be clear, 25–30% of fabric is cut in the manufacturing department [...] therefore, the control on the use of material is adequate. The remaining 70–75% is managed either by external cuts, performed by entities that are only in charge of the cutting activ-ity, or external laboratories that complete the entire cycle. And there, our con-trol can get only up to a certain point [...] Let me just give you a very simple example: if you take a piece of fabric and you measure it, you could say this is 50 meters long; then you try again and then the measure is 50.70 meters. If you measure it another time maybe it is 49.80 meters. If you put it on the wooden

	External work	Value	%
(A)	Budgeted value of external work		100
(B)	Actual value of external work		
(C)	Value of internal work		
(D)=(B)+(C)−(A)	Cost variance		
	From cost variance		
	From volume variance		
(E)	Total costs that cannot be allocated to models		
(D)+(E)	Increase (decrease) of cost		
	Purchases		
(F)	Budgeted value of purchases		100
(G)	Actual value of purchases		
(H)=(G)−(F)	Cost variance		
	From cost variance		
	From volume variance		
(M)	Total costs that cannot be allocated to models		
(M)+(H)	Increase (decrease) of cost		

Figure 6.15   Variance analysis

table you have another measure. The fabric has a certain elasticity, and every time you handle it you can get a different result, therefore you start with the idea that the number of meters that you get is not absolute but there is a certain tolerance. In addition, there are some specific types of fabrics like, for example, jersey, stretch which are by their own nature elastic, much more elastic than the regular fabrics with a flexibility of 6–7–10%. Therefore, in our plan of the production cycle we know that we have to leave the fabric unhandled until the day before to be sure that it is settled [...] It is clear that if 100 meters are needed for production I have to give 100, plus a certain percentage, because this fabric might shrink [...] to this amount of fabric a certain number of units of products is associated. However, there is always a percentage that the company is not able to have under control. And there are also some defects [...] you look at what they might lead in terms of less usage and decide how to avoid waste. This is possible inside the firm but when you go outside, it is very difficult. So there is a certain number of problems that do not allow to have control over real quantities. We refer to historical data, but if a certain laboratory has had a problem, if variances are within a certain range we do not complain, otherwise if they do not convince us, we intervene' *(Technical Director for Italian Activities).*

FirmD prefers closer distances to its suppliers, because a closer distance allows a better monitoring over the manufacturing processes. In this way *FirmD* can control final outputs and behaviours, towards the adherence to technical specifications, quality standards and definite times. In addition, control on financial results is one of the most important determinants for the future of the relationship. *FirmD* needs to know constantly how its partners are doing on the economic side, because their economic performance is unavoidably reflected in *FirmD*'s financial performance. Management accountants are involved in the performance evaluation of the partners, examining the causes and typologies of variances between forecasted and actual data.

The control modes of *FirmD* towards its *façon* producers are very clear, and it seems they perfectly fit in the theoretical patterns.

'Technical control is made through our specialist technicians all over the workshops, at the national level and abroad. Technicians visit very frequently the premises of manufacturers. The principal activity of the technical staff is to evaluate the manufacturer's skills on the production side. They control and approve a first clothing-sample made by the manufacturer, in order to provide him with the authorisation to produce. After that, a control during the production phases occurs, to confirm such skills and capabilities of the manufacturer. The final control is made on the output inside *FirmD*'s laboratories.

The output control process is quite tight: 'hanging items' are severely controlled one by one; for the rest of the items, the packaged ones, sample control is accepted, and the results suggest if the supply meets the quality standards.

On the contrary, the control process toward suppliers is designed on some scheduling, because there are different steps that need tight control. For example, the supplier needs our approval before the dyeing process, because there is a trend of colours. Or, we must know the set-size the supplier applies to items, whether he is following our technical sheet and so on. Another control is made at 75% of the production progress, aimed at verifying the adherence to specifications.

Based on cost per minute standards, we also base our controls on comparing forecasted and actual data. This completes the monitoring process and enables the performance evaluation of the manufacturers. This is one of the most important activities of management accountants' (Technical Director for Foreign Activities).

In addition, *FirmD* manages a series of information services for the agents. Such services are important mechanisms to support sales:

(1) Information on the *warehouse status*: the agent have access to the situation of the finished goods in the warehouse at any time so as to decide when and how to activate re-orders. The re-assortment of the articles takes place during the stores' sales and, within certain limits, the replacement service allows the replacement of unsold items.

(2) *Agent report service*: during the sales campaigns the agent continuously receives information on its sales, the achievement of goals and so on and on the sales of the firm's overall collection. Therefore it is

possible to analyse which products are more successful and which, given low sales opportunities, will never be produced; in this way the agent is able to concentrate his attention on successful products, avoiding the unsuccessful ones.

(3) *Work in progress, production timing*: in this way the agent can monitor the progress of his orders, and is able to provide clear information to his customers.

In *FirmD* the use of information technology is particularly relevant to manage the business and has transformed the way of organising activities. The main functions of information technology are related to managing workshops or *façon* producers and the agents.

Firstly, the workshops are connected, to continuously monitor orders progress and invoices recording. The aim is also to transfer on line the management of the technical sheet and the basic specifications, i.e. the transmission to the workshop of the processing's functional requirements. No information technology-based solutions are adopted for raw materials purchases. Among the basic reasons for this choice is the high turnover of many raw materials providers, which prevents the relationships' stability.

Secondly, all the orders from the agents are managed on-line. In the past the orders were also dealt with by means of applications, based on the classic *electronic data interchange*, but this system had several limits because it was not possible to include all the agents, but only some of them. Today, agents send orders directly to the information system of the firm, by using internet-based solutions, such as IP protocols. All agents are provided with an account (username and password) to connect to the *FirmD's* information system and access a restricted area on the web site.

Table 6.8 summarises the characteristics of the relationships that *FirmD* with its external partners and reports the specifics of management control patterns and accounting information exchanges.

Generalising from a comparative analysis of the case studies: guidelines and recommendations

The theoretical development and the empirical evidence reported in this manuscript suggest some final conclusions on the management accounting and control practices in collaborative relationships.

Table 6.8 Findings on *FirmD*.

Variables and issues	Partners				
	Raw materials suppliers	Façon producers	Finished product suppliers	Agents	
Description of the counterparts	Independent parties that provide *FirmD* with the raw materials, particularly important in the manufacturing process	Putting out. Independent third parties or outsources that are asked to perform some phases or the whole production for *FirmD*	Independent third parties that are asked to complete the entire manufacturing process	Interfirm relationships based on continual interactions	
Relationship life cycle	Temporary to consolidated depending on the type of materials they provide. For materials related to fashion products they are occasional, whereas for consolidated products they are long term	Consolidated, especially with those laboratories that are particularly good and have specific competencies in carrying out a specific activity	Strongly consolidated, especially because of the knowledge of the process related to providing specifications for the manufacturing of the product	Consolidated due to their market knowledge	
Reasons for collaboration	Efficiency and quality of the materials	Stability/predictability of the output generated	Flexibility in the manufacturing process, reducing in this way the risk of sunk investments	Deal with differentiated customers' tastes and customisation	
Governance structure	Market based especially with occasional suppliers	Hierarchy based, in order to guarantee that the activities of the different parties are coordinated	Market based	Market based	

Interdependencies	Sequential interdependencies	High reciprocal interdependence at the network level (different *façonists* can be in charge of carrying out a specific phase and *FirmD* needs to coordinate all the interfaces)	Sequential interdependencies (interdependence is reciprocal only at the initial stage of the process)	Sequential interdependencies
Knowledge on the transformation process	No knowledge of the transformation process	High knowledge on the phase the actor is asked to perform	The principal activity of *FirmD* is to evaluate the manufacturer's skills on the production side. Over time, knowledge on the production process becomes very high	High knowledge of the selling and distribution process but not of the market (sell out)
Output measurability	High measurability of quality standards of raw materials	High output measurability on the manufacturing phase they perform and tight control on the economic results of the single phase	High measurability of operative results according to specifications and of financial results	Medium output measurability
Forms of control	Contractual control: price is the essential element	Prevalence of process control, as adherence to technical specifications is required. Intensive use of ex-ante mechanisms (collaborative planning for technical specifications, timing and costs) and ex post mechanisms (visits to the manufacturing sites of the *façonist*). Output control is also important especially for 'hanging items'	Prevalence of output control based on performance targets but also some process control on progress and compliance with technical specifications	Prevalence of output control

(continued)

Table 6.8 Findings on *FirmD*.

Variables and issues	Partners			
	Raw materials suppliers	Façon producers	Finished product suppliers	Agents
Performance measurement	Quality indicators	Variances analysis, quality indicators, productivity indicators, waste indicators, time indicators (cycle time, delivery time), etc.	Quality indicators, time indicators	Market indicators
Inter-organisational cost management practices (IOCM)	None	No IOCM, price is determined on negotiation basis	Suppliers are involved in the earlier phases of the development processes. IOCM are very important to improve the overall efficiency of manufacturing	None
Cost and management accounting information exchanges	Prices and quantities	Information exchange focus on financial and non-financial data. On the financial side, there are exchanges on costs, prices, profit margins, etc. On the other side, data is mostly about operative processes, as defect rates, spoilage, cycle time, etc.	Information exchanges, except price, regard mostly non-financial information: quantities, cycle time, spoilage, and defect rate	Most information exchanges are in orders collection phase, on sales forecast and effective sales, on the one hand, and work in progress, production timing, on the other

Inter-firm information systems	No IT support in the purchasing side	Information systems are web based and allow parties to access to several information types: work in progress, productive capacity	Parties are integrated through information technology and have reciprocal access to information regarding the progress of manufacturing. There is also a tracking project on orders	Agents are linked to the *FirmD's* information system to submit orders and to verify the state of finished goods warehouse and delivery times
The role of management accounting (MA)	No relevant role	MA has a significant role in defining key measures, based the history of previous relations with the pool of manufacturers	MA has an important role in coordinating and controlling all the activities performed (sample development, manufacturing process, etc.)	No relevant role, apart from collecting market information on sell out

In particular, these conclusions refer to:

- the choice of control modes and the emphasis on collaborative planning;
- the configuration of management accounting information flows, i.e. the design of AINs;
- the management accounting information and tools used in partnerships;
- the role of management accountants.

The choice of control modes and the emphasis on collaborative planning

First of all, the comparative analysis of the case studies highlighted that, despite the several influencing factors indicated by the literature as relevant for control and management accounting practices, there are some of them which are more significant in driving the adoption of specific control patterns and configurations of management accounting information exchanges.

These are:

(1) The *specific governance structure* (Chapter 3) of relationships, i.e. hybrid relationships either characterised by an emphasis on hierarchical or on market-based orientation, as a result of:
    (a) relational asset specificity, deriving from the level of specific and distinctive investments – concerning competencies, procedures, infrastructures, etc. – made by the partners to support the relationship,
    (b) the length of the relationship.
(2) The *interdependence* (Chapter 4) between the partners, as a result of the specific workflows occurring between the partners which may be sequential or reciprocal. This variable needs to be evaluated both at the level of the single relationship and at the networked level. In this last respect, for example, business models involving several partners at different stages of the value chain are characterised by a higher network interdependence than business model where one or two partners take care of most of the activities of the value chain.

The two variables described above can be used to present a framework to provide some *guidelines* and *recommendations* to practitioners on how to choose on the appropriate mix of control mechanisms (Chapter 4) and on how to design management accounting information exchanges (Chapter 5)

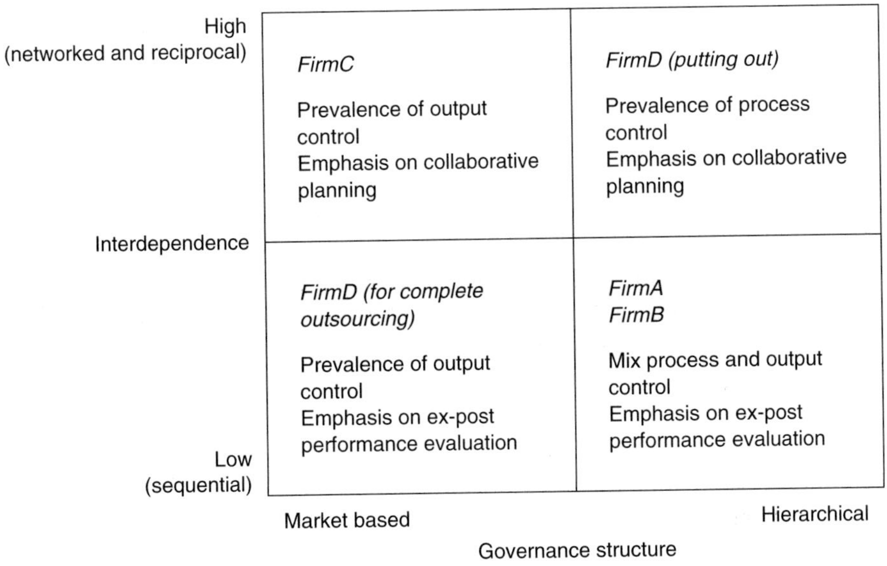

Figure 6.16 Control choices and their determinants in collaboration between firms

on the basis also of the considerations emerging from interpreting and positioning the different cases analysed here (Chapter 6).

Figure 6.16 reports a framework for deciding the adequate form of control in collaboration between firms.

Under relative conditions of low sequential interdependence, in a context of more market-based relationships, the focal firm needs to verify that the activities of the collaborating partners have been carried out according to expectations and the requirements specified in the contract. For this reason, output indicators are predominantly used and regularly monitored ex-post. These refer to quantity produced, mixes of products sold, percentage of units meeting standards, prices and discounts and so on.

In case of collaboration between parties linked by networked reciprocal interdependencies and drawing on market-based relationships, a collaborative planning approach would be appropriate to provide an integrative framework within which overall coordination could take place. This ex-ante definition of goals and expectations would also be complemented by the monitoring of output achievements as a basis for checking the state of the relationship and decide how to revise the joint plans and to manage the future of the relationship accordingly.

When the relationships between partners are characterised by networked reciprocal interdependencies and the collaboration has a hierarchical orientation, an emphasis on collaborative planning is used to manage the processes as efficiently as possible, given that various parties need to coordinate their activities at interfaces. Process control becomes essential to avoid time and cost slippages and is feasible owing to the predominant role of the focal firm which can exercise control both by defining specific process metrics (such as, order completion time, cost of backorder handling, set up time and costs, cost of reworks, number of product delivery delays, ...) and by directly inspecting partners' activities.

In a context where parties are related to each other by sequential interdependencies and relationships are hierarchical in nature, as operations are not characterised by complex links and do not require the intervention of many different actors, they are integrated ex-ante to a lesser extent. In this sense collaborative planning is not particularly sophisticated and crucial for managing the relationship. It is sufficient that the focal firm develops its own plan simply by taking into consideration potential constraints that may derive from the partners. Given this lower emphasis on collaborative plans, to maintain control over the partners, both process and output metrics are adopted in ex-post performance measurement drawing on targets specified by the firm on the basis of past experience.

The four cases described in this chapter represent how these four different modes of control with a higher emphasis on ex-ante planning or ex-post monitoring, and a higher focus on output or process control are enacted in practice, as reported in Figure 6.16.

The design of Accounting Information Networks (AINs)

The analysis of the case studies displayed also that the two variables described above (governance structure and interdependence) can also be used to design the Accounting Information Network existing between the collaborating firms (see Figure 6.17).

In case of collaborations between firms characterised by low interdependence and market-based relationships with partners (as illustrated with reference to *FirmD* for the complete outsourcing relationships), no specific effort and investment is needed to circulate specific management accounting information between the partners. Given the characteristics of operations and the

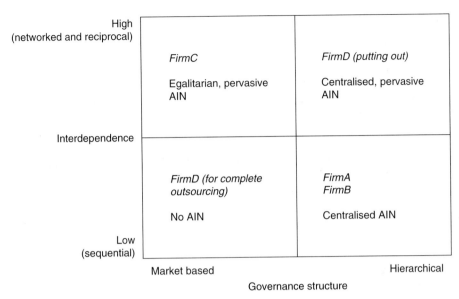

Figure 6.17 The Accounting Information Network (AIN) and its determinants in collaboration between firms

type of relationships, collaboration can be managed by referring to contract specifications and price mechanisms.

When the collaborating firms are in charge of specific activities of the value chain and need to interact with each other to design or complete a specific product (high, networked reciprocal interdependencies), and regulate their transactions through market-based agreements (as illustrated with reference to *FirmC*), collaboration is supported by dense and interconnected management accounting information exchanges. This is because parties need to reciprocally adapt to the requirements and constraints of multiple counterparts, being their contribution critically dependent on the overall contribution of the network.

In this case, the AIN needs to be both high-density, i.e. the number of management accounting information exchanges is to be close to the maximum possible number of them thus to avoid possible information gaps, and high-connectivity, i.e. each party needs to be in contact with a high number of different parties to exchange management accounting information to carry on its operations.

In a context where partners are linked by high, networked reciprocal interdependencies and collaborating relationships are close to hierarchical ones (as illustrated with reference to *FirmD* for the putting out relationships), on the one hand, owing to the nature of interdependence each party has to exchange numerous pieces of management accounting information with several counterparts, on the other hand, the authority and bargaining power of one of the parties leads to a tight control of such party on the type and configuration (i.e. frequency, amount, standards, supports,...) of management accounting information flows.

In this setting, the AIN is highly connected, with one central party playing a key coordinating role of the underlying information flows, because it receives a high number of management accounting pieces of information from all the other parties of the network.

Finally, when the collaborating firms are linked by sequential interdependencies with one party interacting individually with the others, and regulate their transactions through hierarchical agreements agreements (as illustrated with reference to *FirmA* and *FirmB*), collaboration needs to be maintained through the use of centralised management accounting information flows.

In this situation, the AIN needs to be designed to emphasise the coordinating role of the central firm (i.e. the focal one in the network) which operates as a system integrator without the need to maintain dense and interconnected management accounting information flows among the other parties.

In Figure 6.18, we report the graphical representation of the four models of the different AINs where:

Nodes represent the firms involved in the collaborating network. Grey nodes indicate the presence of a central coordinating firm in the AIN.
Arrows represent the management accounting information flows occurring between the parties. The width of rows indicate a higher/lower amount of information exchanged while the direction indicates whether nodes receive or provide management accounting information.

Management accounting information types and the role of management accountants

With the in-depth case studies, we also investigated both the existence of specific interorganisational accounting information flows and the role of management accountants. Evidence showed that despite the fact that partners exchange management accounting information-such as manufacturing

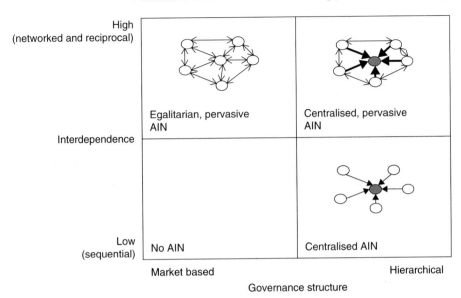

Figure 6.18 The graphical representation of the four AIN models

costs, cost variances, waste/efficiency measures, quality metrics, and cycle time indicators – no specific interorganisational cost technique exists. On the contrary, such information is incorporated within each own partners' control systems. Even when firms use target costing to set and negotiate the prices with their partners, such technique merely represents an extension of an intrafirm practice to an interfirm setting. More generally speaking, the investigated firms use accounting to complement and enhance contract-based relationships thus reducing information asymmetries. This is evident with regard to the following aspects:

(1) Type of information exchanges: communication is based also on cost items and not only price-based arrangements, and agreements refer often to process specifications more than simply output indicators.

(2) Detail of information exchanges: accounting information is frequently beyond the pure price definition and is strictly interconnected with a broader data system that includes other more specific transactions terms like production requirements (timing, quality, delivery and so on), time cycles and medium-term programs for collaborative improvement initiatives.

(3) Time of information exchanges: information is transferred earlier and more frequently than what would happen in a pure market setting.

For example, standard yield rates, scraps, reworks are negotiated and set during the planning process, leading to a more accurate definition of expected results.

In addition, accounting is used as a means by which partners explicitly articulate their differentiated goals and economic perspectives, transcending the need for authority-based coordination. This is suggested by the fact that accounting information exchanges support collaborative planning processes crossing organisational boundaries and sustain the coordination of short-term action plans at the network level as well as the co-definition of medium-term strategic programs.

Finally, data suggested that management accountants are not involved into direct interactions with the partners but it is rather operations managers who directly interact with external parties. Management accountants' main functions, within hybrid environments, have emerged to be:

- supporting operational managers in the economic evaluations of inter-organisational activities;
- coordinating the collection and diffusion of relevant management accounting information with a value-chain focus;
- being responsible for the design and the smooth functioning of information systems as well as for the integrity and consistency of management accounting information and control procedures at the networked level.

To successfully play these roles, management accountants should be therefore exposed to value chain concepts and be sensitised to interorganisational information needs. In this way, they could contribute not only to operational decisions, regarding for example whether products and components should be made in house or not, but also to longer-term strategic decisions such as whether to form a multi-year supply relationship with a specialised partner or to exploit linkages with the partner clients.

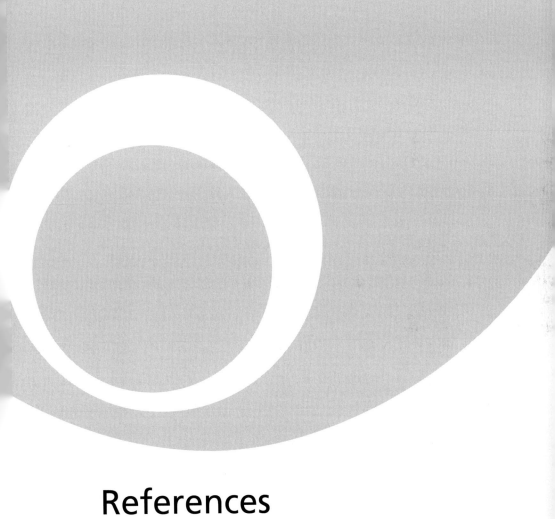

References

Chapter 1

Aldrich, H. E. and Glinov, M. A. (1990). Small world, isn't it? Personal network and infrastructural development. *Paper prepared for the International Technopolis Conference*, San Francisco, 20–22 May.

Baker, G. P., Gibbons, R. and Murphy, K. J. (2002). Relational contracts in strategic alliances. Working Paper. Massachusetts Institute of Technology, Cambridge, MA.

Balcet, G. (1990). Le joint ventures multinazionali: alleanze tra imprese, competizione e potere di mercato economia mondiale. Etas.

Beamish, P. (1988). *Multinational Joint Ventures in Developing Countries.* Routledge.

Bellandi, M. (1986). The Mashallian industrial district. Studi e Discussioni, 42, Department of Economic Science, University of Florence.

Bonacich, P. (1990). Communication dilemmas in social networks: an experimental study. *American Sociological Review*, 5, 448–459.

Bower, J. L. and Rhenman, E. A. (1985). Benevolent cartels. *Harvard Business Review*, 4, 124–132.

Breiger, R. (1981). The social class structure of occupational mobility. *American Journal of Sociology*, 87, 578–611.

Brusco, S. (1982). The Emilian model: productive decentralization and social integration. *Cambridge Journal of Economics*, 6, 167–184.

Burt, R. (1979). A structural theory of interlocking corporate directorates. *Social Networks*, 1, 415–435.

Burt, R. (1980). Cooptive corporate actor networks: a reconsideration of interlocking directorates involving American manufacturing. *Administrative Science Quarterly*, 25, 557–582.

Cainarca, G. C. and Colombo, M. G. (1990). Automazione flessibile, efficienza economica ed organizzazione verticale delle industrie2. *Paper presented at the Conference 'Impresa e contesto competitivo*, Italian Association of Engineers, Milan, 26 October.

D'Aveni, A. (1978). Organizational linkages and resource mobilization: the significance of linkage strength and breadth. *The Sociological Quarterly*, 19, 185–202.

Das, T. K. and Teng, B. S. (2002). Alliance constellations: a social exchange perspective. *Academy of Management Review*, 27, 445–456.

Dioguardi, G. (1987). L'impresa nell'era del computer. IlSole24Ore.

Dioguardi, G. (1990). L'impresa flessibile: una risposta alla competizione globale. *Paper presented at the conference 'Impresa e contesto competitivo'*, Italian Association of Engineers, Milan, 26 October.

Dyer, J. H. (1996). Does governance matter? Keiretsu alliances and asset specificity as sources of Japanese competitive advantage. *Organization Science*, 7, 649–666.

Dyer, J. H. (1997). Effective interfirm collaboration: how firms minimize transaction costs and maximize transaction value. *Strategic Management Journal*, 18, 535–556.

Eccles, R. (1981). The quasifirm in the construction industry. *Journal of Economic Behavior and Organization*, 2, 335–357.

Evan, W. M. and Olk, P. (1990). R&D consortia: A new U.S. organizational form. *Sloan Management Review*, 31, 37–46.

Farrell, J. and Scotchmer, S. (1988). Partnerships. *Quarterly Journal of Economics*, 103, 279–297.

Galaskiewicz, J. (1989). Interorganizational network mobilizing action at the metropolitan level. In *Network of Power* (R. Perucci and H. R. Potter, eds.), pp. 81–96. Aldine de Gruyter.

Gomes-Casseres, B. (1987). Joint venture instability: Is it a problem?. *Columbia Journal of World Business, Summer*, 97–102.

Grandori, A. (1997). An organizational assessment of interfirm coordination modes. *Organization Studies*, 18, 897–925.

Grandori, A. and Soda, G. (1995). Inter-firm networks: antecedents, mechanisms and forms. *Organization Studies*, 16, 183–214.

Granovetter, M. (1985). Economic action and social structure: the problem of embeddedness. *American Journal of Sociology*, 91, 481–510.

Grieco, M. S. and Hosking, D. M. (1987). Networking exchange and skill. *International Studies of Management and Organization*, 17, 75–87.

Gulati, R. and Singh, H. (1998). The architecture of cooperation: managing coordination costs and appropriation concerns in strategic alliances. *Administrative Science Quarterly*, 43, 781–814.

Henderson, J. C. (1990). Plugging into strategic partnerships: the critical IS connection. *Sloan Management Review*, 31, 7–18.

Hennart, J. F. (1988). A transaction costs theory of equity joint ventures. *Strategic Management Journal*, 9, 361–374.

Kieser, A. (1993). Why organization theory needs historical analysis. *Keynote speech at the 11th E.G.O.S. colloquium 'The Production and Diffusion of Managerial Knowledge'*, Paris.

Killing, J. P. (1988). Understanding alliances: the role of task and organizational complexity. In *Cooperative Strategies in International Business* (F. J. Contractor and P. Lorange, eds.), pp. 55–67. Lexington Books.

Lafontaine, F. and Raynaud, E. (2002). Residual claims and self-enforcement as incentive mechanisms in franchise contract: substitutes or complements?. In *The Economics of Contracts* (E. Brousseau and J. M. Glachant, eds.). Cambridge University Press.

Lei, D. and Slocum, J. W. (1990). Global strategic alliances: payoffs and pitfalls. *Organizational Dynamics*, 3, 44–62.

Lorenzoni, G. and Ornati, O. A. (1988). Constellations of firms and new ventures. *Journal of Business Venturing*, 3, 41–57.

Lyles, M. A. (1987). Common mistakes of joint venture experienced firms. *Columbia Journal of World Business*, 22, 78–85.

Mariotti, S. and Cainarca, G. C. (1986). The evolution of transaction governance in the textile-clothing industry. *Journal of Economic Behavior and Organization*, 7, 351–374.

Mariotti, S. and Migliarese, P. (1984). Organizzazione industriale e rapporti tra imprese in un settore ad alto tasso innovativo. *L'Industria*, 1, 71–110.

Ménard, C. (2004). The economics of hybrid organizations. *Journal of Institutional and Theoretical Economics*, 160, 1–32.

Monteverde, K. (1995). Technical dialog as an incentive for vertical integration in the semiconductor industry. *Management Science*, 41, 1624–1638.

Oliver, C. (1990). Determinants of interorganizational relationships: integration and future directions. *The Academy of Management Review*, 15, 241–265.

Oxley, J. E. (1999). Institutional environment and the mechanism of governance: the impact of intellectual property protection on the structure of interfir alliances. *Journal of Economic Behavior and Organization*, 38, 283–309.

Pfeffer, J. and Salancik, G. R. (1978). *The External Control of Organizations: a Resource Dependence Perspective*. Harper and Row.

Pilotti, L. and Pozzana, P. (eds) (1990). *I contratti di franchising: organizzazione e controllo di rete*. Egea: CESCOM Bocconi.

Powell, W. W. (1990). Neither market nor hierarchy: network forms of organization. In *Readings in Organizational Behavior* (L. L. Cummpings and B. Staw, eds.), pp. 295–336. JAI Press.

Powell, W. W. (1996). Inter-organizational collaboration in the biotechnology industry. *Journal of Institutional and Theoretical Economics*, 152, 197–215.

Provan, K. G. (1983). The federation as an interorganizational linkage network. *Academy of Management Review*, 8, 79–89.

Robert, E. B. (1991). High stakes for high-tech entrepreneurs: understanding venture capital decision making. *Sloan Management Review*, 32, 9–21.

Sako, M. and Helper, S. (1998). Determinants of trust in supplier relations: evidence from the automotive industry in Japan and United States. *Journal of Economic Behavior and Organization*, 34, 387–417.

Schrader, S. (1991). Informal technology transfer between firms: cooperation through information trading. *Research Policy*, 2, 153–170.

Shane, S. A. (1996). Hybrid organizational arrangements and their implications for firm. *The Academy of Management Journal*, 39, 216–234.

Soda, G. (1992). Gli accordi di cooperazione inter-organizzativa. In *Osservatorio Organizzativo 1990* (D. Bodega et al., eds.), pp. 69–83. Università Bocconi, Milano.

Staber, U. and Aldrich, H. (1983). Trade association stability and public policy. In *Organizational Theory and Public Policy* (R. Hall and R. Quinn, eds.), pp. 163–178. Sage.

Subramani, M. R. and Henderson, J. C. (1999). The shifting ground between markets and hierarchies: managing a portfolio of relationships. In *The Administrative Evolution* (S. C. Rush and R. N. Katz, eds.). Anker Publishing.

Teece, D. J. (1986). Profiting from technological innovation: implications for integration, collaboration, licensing and public policy. *Research Policy*, 15, 286–305.

Teece, D. J. and Pisano, G. (1994). The dynamic capabilities of firms: an introduction. *Journal of Economic Behavior and Organization*, 3, 556–573.

Turati, C. (1990). *Economia ed organizzazione delle joint venture*. Milan.

Whitley, R. D. (1991). The social construction of business systems in East Asia. *Organization Studies*, 12, 1–28.

Williamson, O. E. (1983). Credible commitments: using hostages to support exchange. *American Economic Review*, 73, 519–540.

Williamson, O. E. (1985). *The Economic Institutions of Capitalism*. Free Press.

Chapter 2

Barney, J. B. (1991). Firm resources and sustained competitive advantage. *Journal of Management*, 17, 99–120.

Cook, K. S. (1977). Exchange and power in networks of interorganizational relations. *The Sociological Quarterly*, 18, 62–82.

Das, T. K. and Teng, B. S. (2000). Instabilities of strategic alliances: an internal tensions perspective. *Organization Science*, 11, 77–101.

Dierickx, I. and Cool, K. (1989). Asset stock accumulation and competitive advantage. *Management Science*, 12, 1504–1511.

DiMaggio, P. J. (1988). Interest and agency in institutional theory. In *Institutional Patterns and Organizations* (L. G. Zucker, eds.), pp. 3–21. Ballinger.

Emerson, R. M. (1962). Power dependence relations. *American Sociological Review*, 27, 31–41.

Galaskiewicz, J. (1985). Interorganizational relations. *Annual Review of Sociology*, 11, 281–304.

Giddens, A. (1984). *The Constitution of Society: Outline of the Theory of Structuration*. University of California Press.

Grandori, A. and Soda, G. (1995). Inter-firm networks: antecedents, mechanisms and forms. *Organization Studies*, 16, 183–214.

Granovetter, M. (1985). Economic action and social structure: the problem of embeddedness. *American Journal of Sociology*, 91, 481–510.

Gulati, R. (1998). Alliances and networks. *Strategic Management Journal*, 19, 293–317.

Gulati, R. (1995). Social structure and alliance formation patterns: a longitudinal analysis. *Administrative Science Quarterly*, 40, 619–652.

Gulati, R. and Singh, H. (1998). The architecture of cooperation: managing coordination costs and appropriation concerns in strategic alliances. *Administrative Science Quarterly*, 43, 781–814.

Gupta, A. K. and Lad, L. J. (1983). Industry self-regulation. An economic, organizational, and political analysis. *Academy of Management Review*, 8, 416–425.

Heide, J. and John, G. (1990). Alliances in industrial purchasing. The determinants of joint action in buyer–supplier relationships. *Journal of Marketing Research*, 28, 24–36.

Inkpen, A. C. (2000). A note on the dynamics of learning alliances: competition, cooperation and relative scope. *Strategic Management Journal*, 21, 775–779.

Ireland, R. D., Hitt, M. A. and Vaidyanath, D. (2002). Alliance management as a source of competitive advantage. *Journal of Management*, 28, 413–446.

Jensen, M. and Meckling, W. (1976). Theory of the firm: managerial behaviour, agency costs, and ownership structure. *Journal of Financial Economics*, 3, 305–360.

Jensen, M. (1983). Organization theory and methodology. *Accounting Review*, 50, 319–339.

Kaneko, I. and Imai, K.i (1987). A network view of the firm. *Paper presented at the 1st Hitostsubashi-Stanford Conference.*

Koenig, T., Gogel, R. and Sonquist, J. (1979). Models of the significance of interlocking corporate directorates. *American Journal of Economics and Sociology*, 38, 173–185.

Kogut, B. and Zander, U. (1992). Knowledge of the firm, combinative capabilities, and the replication of technology. *Organizational Science*, 3, 383–397.

Kotz, D. M. (1978). *Bank Control of Large Corporations in the United States.* University of California Press.

Larson, A. (1992). Network dyads in entrepreneurial settings: a study of governance exchange relationships. *Administrative Science Quarterly*, 37, 76–104.

Madhok, A. (1996). The organization of economic activity: transaction costs, firm capabilities and the nature of governance. *Organization Science*, 7, 577–590.

Madhok, A. (1998). Transaction costs, firm resources and interfirm collaboration. *Paper submitted to the DRUID Summer Conference on Competence,* Governance and Entrepreneurship.

Meyer, J. W. and Rowan, B. (1977). Institutional organizations. Formal structure as myth and ceremony. *American Journal of Sociology*, 83, 340–363.

Oliver, C. (1990). The collective strategy framework. A application to competing predictions of isomorphism. *Administrative Science Quarterly*, 33, 543–561.

Oliver, C. (1990). Determinants of interorganizational relationships: Integration and future directions. *The Academy of Management Review*, 15, 241–265.

Olson, M. Jr. (1982). *The Rise and Decline of Nations. Economic Growth, Stagflation, and Social Rigidities.* Yale University Press.

Ouchi, W. G. (1979). A conceptual framework for the design of organizational control systems. *Management Science*, 25, 833–848.

Palmer, D. (1983). Broken ties interlocking directorates and intercorporate coordination. *Administrative Science Quarterly*, 28, 40–55.

Parkhe, A. (1993). Strategic alliance structuring: a game theoretic and transaction cost examination of interfirm cooperation. *Academy of Management Journal*, 36, 794–829.

Pennings, J. M. (1981). Strategically interdependent organizations. In *Handbook of Organizational Design* (P. C. Nystrom and W. H. Starbuck, eds.), Vol. 1, pp. 433–455. Oxford University Press.

Penrose, E. T. (1959). *The Theory of the Growth of the Firm.* Oxford University Press.

Peteraf, M. (1993). The cornerstones of competitive advantage: a resource-based view. *Strategic Management Journal*, 14, 179–192.

Pfeffer, J. and Salancik, G. R. (1978). *The External Control of Organizations: A Resource Dependence Perspective*. Harper and Row.

Piore, M. J. and Sabel, C. F. (1984). *The Second Industrial Divide*. Basic Books.

Powell, W. W. (1987). Hybrid organizational arrangements: new form or transitional development? *California Management Review*, Fall.

Provan, K. G. (1984). Interorganizational cooperation and decision-making autonomy in a consortium multihospital system. *Academy of Management Review*, 9, 494–504.

Reed, R. and DeFilippi, R. J. (1990). Causal ambiguity, barriers to imitation, and sustainable competitive advantage. *Academy of Management Review*, 15, 88–102.

Schermerhorn, J. R.Jr. (1981). Open questions limiting the practice of interorganizational development. *Group & Organization Studies*, 6, 83–95.

Scott, J. (1985). *Corporations, Classes and Capitalism*. Hutchinson.

Shane, S. A. (1996). Hybrid organizational arrangements and their implications for firm. *The Academy of Management Journal*, 39, 216–234.

Spekman, R. et al. (1988). Alliance management: a view from the past and a look to the future. *Journal of Management Studies*, 35, 747–772.

Stearns, T. M., Hoffman, A. N. and Heide, B. (1987). Performance of commercial television stations as an outcome of interorganizational linkages and environmental conditions. *Academy of Management Journal*, 30, 71–90.

Teece, D. J. (1986). Profiting from technological innovation: implications for integration, collaboration, licensing and public policy. *Research Policy*, 15, 286–305.

Teece, D. J. and Pisano, G. (1994). The dynamic capabilities of firms: an introduction. *Journal of Economic Behavior and Organization*, 3, 556–573.

Teece, D. J., Pisano, G. and Shuen, A. (1997). Dynamic capabilities and strategic management. *Strategic Management Journal*, 18, 509–534.

Thompson, J. D. (1967). *Organization in Action*. McGraw-Hill.

Warren, R. L. (1967). The interorganizational field as a focus for investigation. *Administrative Science Quarterly*, 12, 396–419.

Whetten, D. A. (1978). Coping with incompatible expectations. An integrated view of role conflict. *Administrative Science Quarterly*, 23, 254–271.

Whetten, D. A. (1981). Interorganizational relations. A review of the field. *Journal of Higher Education*, 52, 1–28.

Wievel, W. and Hunter, A. (1985). The interorganizational network as a resource. A comparative case study on organizational genesis. *Administrative Science Quarterly*, 30, 482–496.

Williamson, O. E. (1985). *The Economic Institutions of Capitalism*. Free Press.

Williamson, O. E. (1991). Comparative economic organization: the analysis of discrete structural alternatives. *Administrative Science Quarterly*, 36, 269–296.

Zeitz, G. (1980). Interorganizational dialectics. *Administrative Science Quarterly*, 25, 72–88.

Zucker, L. G. (1977). The role of institutionalization in cultural persistence. *American Sociological Review*, 42, 726–743.

Chapter 3

Aldrich, H. E. and Whetten, D. A. (1981). Organization-sets, action-sets, and networks: making the most of simplicity. In *Handbook of Organizational Design* (P. C. Nystrom and H. Starbuck, eds.), pp. 385–408. Oxford University Press.

Amigoni, F., Caglio, A. and Ditillo, A. (2003). Dis-integration through integration: the emergence of accounting information networks. In *Management Accounting in the Digital Economy* (A. Bhimani, eds.), pp. 17–35. Oxford University Press.

Arrow, K. J. (1974). *The Limits of Organization*. Norton.

Berry, L. (2000). *The Consequences of Inter-firm Supply Chains for Management accounting*. The Chartered Institute of Management Accountants.

Borys, B. and Jemison, D. B. (1989). Hybrid arrangements as strategic alliances: theoretical issues in organizational combinations. *The Academy of Management Review*, 14(2), 234–249.

Bradach, J. L. and Eccles, R. G. (1989). Price, authority, and trust: from ideal types to plural forms. *Annual Review of Sociology*, 15, 97–118.

Chandler, A. D. Jr. (1984). The emergence of managerial capitalism. *Business History Review*, 58, 473–503.

Coase, R. H. (1937). The nature of the firm. *Economica, New Series*, 4(16), 386–405.

Coase, R. H. (1960). The problem of social cost. *Journal of Law and Economics*, 3(October), 1–44.

Commons, J. R. (1934). *Institutional Economics*. University of Wisconsin Press.

Cooper, R. and Slagmulder, R. (1999). *Supply Chain Development for the Lean Enterprise*. Productivity.

Daems, H. (1983). The determinants of the hierarchical organization of industry. In *Power, Efficiency and Institutions* (A. Francis et al., eds.), pp. 35–53. Heinemann.

Ebers, M. (1999). *The Formation of Inter-Organizational Networks*. Oxford University Press.

Gomes-Casseres, B. (1994). Group versus group: how alliance networks compete. *Harvard Business Review*, July–August, 4–11.

Grandori, A. and Soda, G. (1995). Inter-firm networks: antecedents, mechanisms and forms. *Organization Studies*, 16(2), 183–214.

Granovetter, M. (1985). Economic action and social structure: the problem of embeddedness. *American Journal of Sociology*, 91, 481–510.

Griesinger, D. W. (1990). The human side of economic organization. *The Academy of Management Review*, 15(3), 478–499.

Hennart, J. F. (1993). Explaining the swollen middle: why most transactions are a mix of 'market' and 'hierarchy'. *Organization Science*, 4(4), 529–547.

Holland, C. P. and Lockett, A. G. (1997). Mixed mode network structures: the strategic use of electronic communication by organizations. *Organization Science*, 8(5), 475–488.

Lorenz, E. H. (1988). Neither friends nor strangers: informal networks of subcontracting in French industry. In *Trust: Making or Breaking Cooperative Relations* (D. Gambetta, eds.), pp. 194–210. Basil Blackwell.

March, J. G. and Simon, H. A. (1958). *Organizations*. Wiley.

Mathewson, G. F. and Winer, R. A. (1985). The economics of franchise contracts. *Journal of Law and Economics*, 28, 503–526.

Ménard, C. (2004). The economics of hybrid organizations. *Journal of Institutional and Theoretical Economics*, 160, 1–32.

Nohria, N. and Eccles, R. G. (eds.) (1992). *Networks and Organizations*. Harvard Business School Press.

Ouchi, W. G. (1978). The transmission of control through organizational hierarchy. *Academy of Management Journal*, 21, 173–192.

Ouchi, W. G. (1980). Markets, bureaucracies, and clans. *Administrative Science Quarterly*, 25(1), 129–141.

Palay, T. M. (1984). Comparative institutional economics: the governance of rail freight contracting. *The Journal of Legal Studies*, 13(2), 265–287.

Pfeffer, J. and Salancik, G. R. (1978). *The External Control of Organizations: A Resource Dependence Perspective*. Harper and Row.

Powell, W. W. (1990). Neither market nor hierarchy: network forms of organization. *Research in Organizational Behavior*, 12, 295–336.

Ring, P. S. and Van de Ven, A. (1992). Structuring cooperative relationships between organizations. *Strategic Management Journal*, 13, 483–498.

Ring, P. S. and Van de Ven, A. (1994). Developmental processes of cooperative interorganizational relationships. *Academy of Management Review*, 19, 90–118.

Scott, W. R. (1987). *Organizations: Rational, Natural and Open Systems*. Prentice Hall.

Stinchcombe, A. L. (1985). Contracts as hierarchical documents. In *Organizational Theory and Project Management: Administering Uncertainty in Norwegian Offshore Oil* (A. L. Stinchcombe and C. A. Heimer, eds.). Norwegian University Press.

Subramani, M. R. and Henderson, J. C. (1999). The shifting ground between markets and hierarchies: managing a portfolio of relationships. In *The Administrative Evolution* (S. C. Rush and R. N. Katz, eds.). Anker Publishing.

Tomkins, C. (2001). Interdependencies, trust and information in relationships, alliances and networks. *Accounting, Organizations and Society*, 26, 161–191.

Turnbull, P. W. and Valla, J. P. (eds.) (1986). *Strategies for International Industrial Marketing: The Management of Customer Relationships in European Industrial Markets*. Croom Helm.

Uzzi, B. (1996). The sources and consequences of embeddedness for the economic performance of organizations: the network effect. *American Sociological Review*, 61(4), 674–698.

Williamson, O. E. (1975). *Markets and hierarchies: analysis and antitrust implications*. Free Press.

Williamson, O. E. (1981). The economics of organization: the transaction cost approach. *The American Journal of Sociology*, 87(3), 548–577.

Williamson, O. E. (1985). *The Economic Institutions of Capitalism*. The Free Press.

Williamson, O. E. (1991). Comparative economic organization: the analysis of discrete structural alternatives. *Administrative Science Quarterly*, 36(1), 269–296.

Williamson, O. E. (1994). Transaction cost economics and organization theory. In *The Handbook of Economic Sociology* (N. J. Smelser and R. Swedberg, eds.), pp. 77–107. Princeton University Press.

Williamson, O. E. (1996). *The Mechanisms of Governance.* Oxford University Press.

Zaheer, A. and Venkatraman, N. (1995). Relational governance as an inter-organizational strategy: an empirical test of the role of trust in economic exchange. *Strategic Management Journal*, 16(5), 373–392.

Zaheer, A. and Venkatraman, N. (1994). Determinants of electronic integration in the insurance industry: an empirical test. *Management Science*, 40(5), 549–566.

Zenger, T. R. and Hesterly, W. S. (1997). The disaggregation of corporations: selective intervention, high-powered incentives, and molecular units. *Organization Science*, 8(3), 209–222.

Chapter 4

Alchian, A. A. and Demsetz, H. (1972). Production, information costs and economic organization. *American Economic Review*, 62, 777–795.

Avadikian, A., Cohendet, P. and Llerena, P. (1993). Coherence, diversity of assets and networks. *ESF-EMOT Conference. Coping with Complexity and Diversity of Assets, and Learning and Adapting to Strategic Change*, Strasbourg.

Baliga, B. R. and Jaeger, A. M. (1984). Multinational corporations: control systems and delegation issues. *Journal of International Business Studies*, 15, 25–40.

Birnbirg, J. (1998). Control in interfirm co-operative relationships. *Journal of Management Studies*, 35, 421–428.

Blodgett, L. L. (1991). Partner contributions as predictors of equity share in international joint ventures. *Journal of International Business Studies*, 22, 63–78.

Bradach, J. L. and Eccles, R. G. (1989). Price, authority, and trust: from ideal types to plural forms. *Annual Review of Sociology*, 15, 97–118.

Child, J. (1972). Organizational structure, environment and performance: the role of strategic choice. *Sociology*, 6, 2–22.

Coletti, A. L., Sedatole, K. L. and Towry, K. L. (2005). The effect of control systems on trust and cooperation in collaborative environments. *The Accounting Review*, 80, 477–500.

Cyr, D. J. and Schneider, S. C. (1996). Implications for learning: human resource management in East–West joint ventures. *Organization Studies*, 17, 207–226.

Das, T. K. and Teng, B. (1996). Risk types and inter-firm alliance structures. *Journal of Management Studies*, 33, 827–843.

Das, T. K. and Teng, B. S. (1998). *Academy of Management Review*, 23, 491–512.

Das, T. K. and Teng, B. S. (2001a). Trust, control, and risk in strategic alliances: an integrated framework. *Organization Studies*, 22, 251–283.

Das, T. K. and Teng, B. S. (2001b). A risk perception model of alliance structuring. *Journal of International Management*, 7, 1–29.

Dekker, H. C. (2004). Control of inter-organizational relationships: evidence on appropriation concerns and coordination requirements. *Accounting, Organizations and Society*, 29, 27–49.

Dyer, J. H. (1996). Specialized supplier networks as a source of competitive advantage: evidence from the auto industry. *Strategic Management Journal*, 17, 271–291.

Edstrom, A. and Galbraith, J. (1977). Transfer of managers as coordination and control strategy in multinational organizations. *Administrative Science Quarterly*, 22, 248–263.

Eisenhardt, K. M. (1985). Control: organizational and economic approaches. *Management Science*, 31, 134–149.

Etzioni, A. (1961). *A Comparative Analysis of Complex Organizations: On Power, Involvement, and Their Correlates*. Free Press.

Etzioni, A. (1965). Organizational control structure. In *Handbook of Organizations* (J. G. March, ed.), pp. 650–677. Rand McNally.

Fama, E. F. and Jensen, M. (1983). Agency problems and residual claims. *Journal of Law and Economics*, 26, 327–349.

Flamholtz, E. G., Das, T. K. and Tsui, A. S. (1985). Toward and integrative framework of organizational control. *Accounting, Organizations and Society*, 10, 35–50.

Galbraith, J. R. (1977). *Organization Design*. Addison Wesley.

Garcia-Canal, E. (1996). Contractual form in domestic and international strategic alliances. *Organization Studies*, 17, 773–794.

Geringer, J. M. and Hebert, L. (1989). Control and performance of international joint ventures. *Journal of International Business Studies*, 20, 235–254.

Giglioni, G. B. and Bedeian, A. B. (1974). A conspectus of management control theory: 1900–1972. *Academy of Management Journal*, 17, 292–305.

Grandori, A. (1997). An organizational assessment of interfirm coordination modes. *Organization Studies*, 18, 897–925.

Green, S. and Welsh, M. A. (1988). Cybernetics and dependence: reframing the control concept. *Academy of Management Review*, 13, 287–301.

Groot, T. L. C. M. and Merchant, K. A. (2000). *Accounting, Organizations and Society*, 25, 579–607.

Gulati, R. and Singh, H. (1998). *The Architecture of Cooperation: Managing Coordination Costs and Appropriation Concerns in Strategic Alliances. Aministrative Science Quartely*, 43, 781–814.

Harrigan, K. R. (1988). Joint ventures and competitive strategy. *Strategic Management Journal*, 9, 141–158.

Heide, J. B. (1994). Interorganizational governance in marketing channels. *Journal of Marketing*, 58, 71–85.

Killing, J. P. (1988). Understanding alliances: the role of task and organizational complexity. In *Cooperative Strategies in International Business* (F. J. Contractor and P. Lorange, eds.), pp. 56–68. Lexington Books.

Kirsch, L. J. (1996). The management of complex tasks in organizations: controlling the systems development process. *Organization Science*, 7, 1–21.

Lewis, J. (1995). *The Connected Corporation*. Free Press.

Littler, D. and Leverick, F. (1995). Joint ventures for product development: learning from experience. *Long Range Planning*, 28, 58–67.

Lorange, P. and Morton, M. S. Scott (1974). A framework for management control systems. *Sloan Management Review*, Fall, 41–56.

Makhija, M. V. and Ganesh, U. (1997). The relationship between control and partner learning in learning-related joint ventures. *Organization Science*, 8, 508–527.

March, J. G. and Simon, H. A. (1958). *Organizations*. Wiley.

Merchant, K. A. (1982). The control function of management. *Sloan Management Review*, 23, 43–55.

Mintzberg, H. (1979). *The Structuring of Organizations*. Prentice-Hall.

Nonaka, I. (1994). A dynamic theory of organizational knowledge creation. *Organization Science*, 5, 14–37.

Noteboom, B. (1996). Trust, opportunism and governance: a process and control model. *Organization Studies*, 17, 985–1010.

Ouchi, W. G. (1978). The transmission of control through organizational hierarchy. *Academy of Management Journal*, 21, 173–192.

Ouchi, W. G. (1979). A conceptual framework for the design of organizational control systems. *Management Science*, 25, 833–848.

Ouchi, W. G. (1980). Markets, bureaucracies and clans. *Administrative Science Quarterly*, 25, 129–141.

Ouchi, W. G. and Maguire, M. A. (1975). Organizational control; two functions. *Administrative Science Quarterly*, 20, 559–569.

Perrow, C. (1967). A framework for the comparative analysis of organization. *American Sociology Review*, 32, 194–208.

Ring, P. S. and Van de Ven, A. (1992). Structuring cooperative relationships between organizations. *Strategic Management Journal*, 13, 483–498.

Rousseau, D. M. et al. (1998). Not so different after all: a cross-discipline view of trust. *Academy of Management Journal*, 38, 7–23.

Schaan, J. L. F. (1983). Parent control and joint venture success: the case of Mexico. Unpublished doctoral dissertation. University of Western Ontario, Canada.

Schreyogg, G. and Steinmann, H. (1987). *The Academy of Management Review*, 12, 91–103.

Simons, R. (1991). Strategic orientation and top management attention to control systems. *Strategic Management Journal*, 12, 49–62.

Subramani, M. R. and Henderson, J. C. (1999). A typology of hybrid governance: proposal and empirical validation. *Paper presented at the Academy Management Conference*, Business Policy and Strategy (BPS) Division, Chicago, IL.

Sydow, J. and Windeler, A. (1998). Organizing and evaluating interfirm networks: a structurationist perspective on the network processes and effectiveness. *Organization Science*, 9, 265–268.

Tannembaum, A. (1968). *Control in Organizations*. McGraw-Hill.

Teece, D. J. (1992). Competition, cooperation, and innovation: organizational arrangements for regimes of rapid technological progress. *Journal of Economic Behavior and Organization*, 18, 1–25.

Thompson, J. D. (1967). *Organizations in Action*. McGraw-Hill.

Tomkins, C. (2001). Interdependencies, trust and information in relationships, alliances and networks. *Accounting, Organizations and Society*, 26, 161–191.

Van der Meer-Kooistra, J. and Vosselman, E. G. J. (2000). Management control of interfirm transactional relationships: the case of industrial renovation and maintenance. *Accounting, Organizations and Society*, 25, 51–77.

Vancil, R. F. (1979). *Decentralization: Managerial Ambiguity by Design*. Dow Jones.

Varian, H. R. (1990). Monitoring agents with other agents. *Journal of Institutional and Theoretical Economics*, 146, 153–174.

von Hippel, E. (1994). 'Sticky information' and the locus of problem solving: implications for innovation. *Management Science*, 40, 429–439.

West, M. W. (1959). Thinking ahead. The jointly owned subsidiary. *Harvard Business Review*, 37, 165–172.

Williamson, O. E. (1981). The economics of organization: the transaction cost approach. *American Journal of Sociology*, 87, 548–577.

Yan, A. and Gray, B. (1994). Bargaining power, management control, and performance in United States–China joint ventures: a comparative case study. *Academy of Management Journal*, 37, 1478–1517.

Yoshino, M. and Rangan, U. S. (1995). *Strategic Alliances: An Entrepreneurial Approach to Globalization*. Harvard Business School Press.

Chapter 5

Amigoni, F., Caglio, A. and Ditillo, A. (2003). Dis-integration through integration: the emergence of accounting information networks. In *Management Accounting in the Digital Economy* (A. Bhimani, ed.). Oxford University Press.

Andraski, J. (2003). CPFR emerges as the next movement in supply chain management. In *Collaborative Planning, Forecasting, and Replenishment – How to Create a Supply Chain Advantage* (D. Seifert, ed.), pp. 56–70. New York. American Management Association.

Andraski, J. C. and Yeso, M. D. (2003). The power of standards based collaboration – The Uniform Code Council and CPFR. In *Collaborative Planning, Forecasting, and Replenishment – How to Create a Supply Chain advantage* (D. Seifert, ed.), pp. 162–172. New York. American Management Association.

Atkinson, A. and Waterhouse, J. (1996). *Strategic performance measurement: scope and implementation issues*. Working paper. University of Waterloo.

Baiman, S., Fischer, P. E. and Rajan, M. V. (1998). *Information, contracting, and quality costs. Working paper*. University of Pennsylvania.

Bavelas, A. (1951). Communication patterns in Task-oriented groups. In *The Policy Sciences* (D. Lerner and H. K. Lasswell, eds.). Stanford. Stanford University Press,

Brewer, P. C. and Speh, T. W. (2000). Using the balanced scorecard to measure supply chain performance. *Journal of Business Logistics*, 21(1), 75–94.

Carr, L. P. and Ittner, C. D. (1992). Measuring the cost of ownership. *Journal of Cost Management*, Fall, 42–51.

Chapman, C. (1998). Accountants in organizational networks. *Accounting, Organizations and Society*, 23(8), 737–766.

Coad, A. F. and Cullen, J. (2006). Inter-organisational cost management: towards an evolutionary perspective. *Management Accounting Research*, 17, 342–369.

Cooper, R. and Slagmulder, R. (1999). *Supply Chain Development for the Lean Enterprise*. Productivity.

Cooper, R. and Slagmulder, R. (2003). Interorganizational costing, Part 1. *Cost Management*, September/October, 14–21.

Cooper, R. and Slagmulder, R. (2003). Interorganizational costing, Part 2. *Cost Management*, November/December, 12–24.

Cooper, R. and Slagmulder, R. (2004). Interorganizational cost management and relational context. *Accounting, Organizations and Society*, 29, 1–26.

Degraeve, Z., Labro, E. and Roodhooft, F. (2000). An evaluation of vendor selection models from a total cost of ownership perspective. *European Journal of Operational Research*, 125, 34–58.

Degraeve, Z., Labro, E. and Roodhooft, F. (2004). Constructing a total cost of ownership supplier selection methodology based on activity based costing and mathematical programming. Vlerick Leuven Gent Working Paper Series.

Dekker, H. C. (2003). Value chain analysis in interfirm relationships: a field study. *Management Accounting Research*, 14, 1–23.

Dekker, H. C. (2004). Control of inter-organizational relationships: evidence on appropriation concerns and coordination requirements. *Accounting, Organizations and Society*, 29, 27–49.

Dekker, H. and Van Goor, A. R. (2000). Supply chain management and management accounting: a case study of activity-based costing. *International Journal of Logistics, Research and Applications*, 3(1), 41–52.

Ellram, L. M. (1995). Activity-based costing and total cost of ownership: a critical linkage. *Journal of Cost Management*, Winter, 22–30.

Ellram, L. M. and Siferd, S. P. (1995). Total cost of ownership: a key concept in strategic cost management decisions. *Journal of Business Logistics*, 19(1), 55–84.

Ellram, L. M. (1993). Total cost of ownership: elements and implementation. *International Journal of Purchasing and Materials Management*, Fall, 3–11.

Ellram, L. M. and Siferd, S. P. (1998). Total cost of ownership: a key concept in strategic cost management decisions. *Journal of Business Logistics*, 19(1), 55–76.

Fennell, L. E. (2003). Consumer-centric CPFR. In *Collaborative Planning, Forecasting, and Replenishment – How to Create a Supply Chain Advantage* (D. Seifert, ed.), pp. 111–122. American Management Association, New York.

Frazier, G. L., Spekman, R. E. and O'Neal, C. R. (1988). Just in time exchange relationships in industrial markets. *Journal of Marketing*, 52, 52–67.

Freeman, L. C., Roeder, D. and Mulholland, R. R. (1980). Centrality in social networks. II. Experimental results. *Social Networks*, 2, 119–141.

Gietzmann, M. B. (1996). Incomplete contracts and the make or buy decision: governance design and attainable flexibility. *Accounting, Organizations and Society*, 21(6), 611–626.

Griffin, A. and Hauser, J. R. (1996). Integrating R&D and marketing: a review and analysis of the literature. *Journal of Product Innovation Management*, 13(3), 191–215.

Guilding, C., Cravens, K. S. and Tayles, M. (2000). An international comparison of strategic management accounting practices. *Management Accounting Research*, 11, 113–135.

Håkansson, H. and Lind, J. (2007). Accounting in an interorganizational setting. In Chapman, C. S., Hoppwood, A. J., Shields M. D. (eds.), *Handbook of Management Accounting Research*, vol. 2, pp. 885–902, Elsevier.

Handfield, R. B. and Nichols, E. L. (1999). *Introduction to Supply Chain Management*. Harlow: England.

Hines, P., Lamming, R., Jones, D., Cousins, P. and Rich, N. (2000). *Value Stream – Management Strategy and Excellence in the Supply Chain*. Financial Times Prentice Hall.

Holmstrom, J., Framling, K., Kaipia, R. and Saranen, J. (2002). Collaborative planning, forecasting and replenishment – new solutions needed for mass collaboration. *Supply Chain Management: An International Journal*, 7(3), 136–145.

Ittner, C. D., Larcker, D. F., Nagar, V. and Rajan, M. V. (1999). Supplier selection, monitoring practices, and firm performance. *Journal of Accounting and Public Policy*, 18, 253–281.

Kajüter, P. and Kulmala, H. (2005). Open-book accounting in networks. Potential achievements and reasons for failures. *Management Accounting Research*, 16(2), 179–204.

Kenneth, J. P., Gary, L. R. and Robert, M. M. (2005). An examination of collaborative planning effectiveness and supply chain performance. *The Journal of Supply Chain Management*, 41(2), 14–25.

Krishnaprasad, G. B. R. (2003). CPFR and its applicability to industry. *The Management Accountant*, 38(7), 500–501.

Kulmala, H. I. (2002). Accounting in customer–supplier relationships. Developing cost management in network environment. *Proceedings of the 3rd Conference on New Directions in Management Accounting: Innovations in Practice and Research*, 2, 699–716.

LaLonde, B. and Pohlen, T. (1996). Issues in supply chain costing. *The International Journal of Logistics Management*, 7(1), 1–12.

Lamming, R. (1993). *Beyond Partnership: Strategies for Innovation and Lean Supply*. Prentice Hall.

Marquez, A. C., Bianchi, C. and Gupta, J. N. D. (2004). Operational and financial effectiveness of e-collaboration tools in supply chain integration. *European Journal of Operational Research*, 159, 348–363.

Mecimore, C. D. and Bell, A. T. (1995). Are we ready for fourth-generation ABC? *Management Accounting*, January, 22–26.

Mouritsen, J., Hansen, A. and Hansen, C.Ø. (2001). Inter-organizational controls and organizational competencies: episodes around target cost management/ functional analysis and open book accounting. *Management Accounting Research*, 12, 221–244.

Munday, M. (1992). Accounting cost data disclosure and buyer–supplier partnerships: a research note. *Management Accounting Research*, 3(3), 245–250.

Noordewier, T. G., John, G. and Nevin, J. (1990). Performance outcomes of purchasing arrangements in industrial buyer–vendor relationships. *Journal of Marketing*, 54(4), 80–93.

Porter, M. E. (1985). *Competitive Advantage*. Upper Saddle River: The Free Press, Prentice Hall.

Riley, D. (1987). *Competitive cost based investment strategies for industrial companies. Manufacturing issues*. Booz, Allen, and Hamilton.

Saha, P. (2007). Factors Influencing Broad Based CPFR® Adoption, Working paper.

Sawhney, M. and Parikh, D. (2001). Where value lives in a networked world. *Harvard Business Review*, January, 79–86.

Schmitz, J. and Platts, K. Supplier Logistics Performance Measurement in the Automotive Industry. Working Paper. University of Cambridge.

Seal, W. B., Cullen, J., Dunlop, A., Berry, A. and Mirghani, A. (1999). Enacting a European supply chain: the role of management accounting. *Management Accounting Research*, 10, 303–322.

Shank, J. K. (1989). Strategic cost management: new wine, or just new bottles?. *Management Accounting Research*, 1, 47–65.

Shank, J. K. and Govindarajan, V. (1992). Strategic cost management: the value chain perspective. *Management Accounting Research*, 4, 177–197.

Shank, J. K. and Govindarajan, V. (1993). *Strategic Cost Management*. The Free Press.

Soda, G. (1998). *Reti tra imprese* Roma, Carocci Editore.

Stump, R. L. and Heide, J. B. (1996). Controlling supplier opportunism in industrial relationships. *Journal of Marketing Research*, 33(1), 431–441.

Voluntary Interindustry Commerce Standards Association (2002). Collaborative Planning, Forecasting and Replenishment Version 2.0. Available at http://www.cpfr.org.

Wasserman, S. and Faust, K. (1994). *Social Network Analysis: Methods and Applications.* Cambridge, UK: Cambridge University Press.

Weisphal, N., Pfahler, W. and Abolhassan, F. (2003). Results of a CPFR study in Europe. In *Collaborative Planning, Forecasting, and Replenishment – How to Create a Supply Chain Advantage* (D. Seifert, ed.), pp. 176–203. American Management Association, New York.

Wouters, M., Anderson, J. C. and Wynstra, F. (2005). The adoption of total cost of ownership for sourcing decisions – a structural equation analysis. *Accounting, Organizations and Society*, 30, 167–191.

Zhenxin, Y., Hong Yan, T. C. and Cheng, E. (2001). Benefits of information sharing with supply chain partnerships. *Industrial Management & Data Systems*, 101(3), 114–121.

Zimmermann, K. (2003). Using the balanced scorecard for interorganizational performance management of supply chains – a case study. In *Cost Management in Supply Chains* (S. Seuring and M. Goldbach, eds.), pp. 399–415. Physica, Heidelberg.

Chapter 6

De, W. B. and Meyer, R. (2004). Network strategy. In *Strategy: Process, Content and Context* (W. B. De and R. Meyer, eds.). Thomson Learning.

Lorenzoni, G. and Baden-Fuller, C. (1995). Creating a strategic center to manage a web of partners. *California Management Review*, 37, 3.

Index